ODDBALL
IOWA

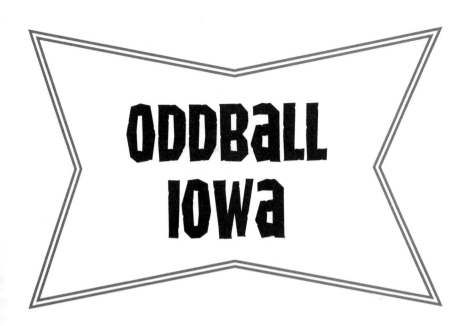

ODDBALL IOWA

A Guide to Some Really
STRANGE PLACES

JEROME POHLEN

CHICAGO REVIEW PRESS

The author has made every effort to secure permissions for all the material in this book. If any acknowledgment has inadvertently been omitted, please contact the author.

All photographs courtesy of Jerome Pohlen unless otherwise noted.

Cover and interior design: Mel Kupfer

First Edition
Published by Chicago Review Press, Incorporated
814 North Franklin Street
Chicago, Illinois 60610
ISBN 1-55652-564-8
Printed in the United States of America
5 4 3 2 1

FOR UNCLE ALVIN,
AUNT SUE, THERESA,
MARY, MIKE, JOAN,
AND DAN

CONTENTS

INTRODUCTION ix

1. THE NORTHWEST 1
   Map of the Northwest. 60–61

2. THE NORTHEAST 63
   Map of the Northeast 108–109

4. THE SOUTHWEST 111
   Map of the Southwest. 142–143

6. THE SOUTHEAST 145
   Map of the Southeast 184–185

7. THE CELEBRITIES IN TROUBLE TOUR 187

EPILOGUE 201

ACKNOWLEDGMENTS 203

RECOMMENDED SOURCES 205

INDEX BY CITY NAME 211

INDEX BY SITE NAME 221

INtRODUCtiON

*T*he good folks at the Iowa Tourism Office would like you to know that their state has more to offer visitors than corn, pigs, and more corn. Iowa has stunning Mississippi River bluffs, impressive art museums, scenic rivers and byways, and historic ethnic communities. Yes, Iowa is a Grant Wood painting come to life: small-town America populated by the salt of the earth.

But this isn't a book about all *that*.

What is it about? The future birthplace of Captain James T. Kirk. The annual Hobo Convention. The Winterset outhouse listed on the National Register of Historic Places. It's about the butter sculptures at the Iowa State Fair, the World's Largest Cheeto, the Estherville meteorite, and the "Lonely Goatherder" marionettes from *The Sound of Music*. It's about Le Mars, the Ice Cream Capital of the World, and Macksburg, host of the annual National Skillet Throw. It's about all those places you'd rather spend your weekends than those oh-so-quaint Amana Colonies.

And for all you readers who need to feel you've learned a thing or two before you're done, *Oddball Iowa* is chock-full of important state history. Did you know that Ozzy Osbourne's infamous bat-biting incident took place in Iowa? It's true! Or that Bonnie and Clyde almost came to a bloody end here, just down the road from where Jesse James pulled his first moving train robbery? Yep. Iowa is also the birthplace of the Roto-Rooter, the Delicious apple, the electronic computer, the reinforced concrete bridge, and the Eskimo Pie.

What, is all this *news* to you? It shouldn't be: Iowa has the nation's highest literacy rate (99 percent), the highest per capita population with undergraduate degrees, and the highest average combined SAT scores. So why do so few residents know that Iowa is home to the world's shortest and steepest inclined railway? Or that the state is a leader in Invincible Defense Technology? Or that Iowa's best museum is a one-room collection of scale models built entirely out of matchsticks? This drought of weird information must end. This is why *Oddball Iowa* is so critically important.

While I've tried to give clear directions from major roads and landmarks, you could still make a wrong turn. When the corn gets yay high—I'm now holding my hand level with my forehead—it's sometimes difficult to see where you're going. Here are a few Oddball travel tips to help you reach your destination:

➡ **Stop and ask!** I travel a lot, and Iowa is the only state in the nation where I was given clear, concise, and *correct* directions every time I asked. Maybe folks are just smarter here. Maybe it's because the state is laid out in a gigantic, mile-road grid. Or maybe everyone in Iowa knows a whole lot more about everyone else's business than they really should. Whatever the reason, you're the ultimate beneficiary, as long as you suck up your pride, pull over, and *ask.*

➡ **Call ahead.** Few Oddball sites keep truly regular hours. Many Iowa attractions are only open in the afternoon, after the chores are done, but before the tornados send everyone running for the cellars. Always call. And if you spot a tornado, grab your camcorder and look for a low-lying ditch.

➡ **Don't give up.** Think of the farmer who built that small museum when he wasn't busy putting food on the table for the whole world. He made the extra effort. Shouldn't you?

➡ **Don't trespass!** Don't become a Terrible Tourist. If one of the sites in this book is not open to the public, stay on the road. Besides, you don't want to step in something, and believe me, there's lots of "something" out there.

Do you have an Oddball site of your own? Have I missed anything? Do you know of a location that should be included in a later edition? Please write and let me know: c/o Chicago Review Press, 814 N. Franklin Street, Chicago, IL 60610.

ODDBALL IOWA

THE NOrtHWest

Why don't we start at the top and work our way down? Northwest Iowa's Hawkeye Point, near Sibley, could be considered the "top" of Iowa, soaring 1,670 feet above sea level. It's not as enticing to mountain climbers as, say, Pikes Peak or Mount Rainier since most of the land around it is 1,660-something feet above sea level, but for burger-with-fries lovers, a brisk hike to the summit is just what the doctor ordered. OK, *part* of what the doctor ordered. . . .

Hawkeye Point isn't the only record-breaking tourist destination in Iowa's northwest quadrant. The region is also home to the World's Largest Grotto, the World's First Digital Computer, the World's Largest Ice Cream Factory, the World's Longest Double-Track Train Trestle, the World's Largest Bull, the World's Largest Bullhead, the World's First Reinforced Concrete Bridge, the World's Largest Pocahontas Statue, the World's First Moving Train Robbery, and, best of all, the World's Largest Cheeto!

What—you need *more* reasons to visit? Then read on.

Hell countryside.

Adair
World's First Moving Train Robbery

Good ol' American ingenuity! When the James–Younger Gang derailed the Chicago, Rock Island & Pacific train near Adair on July 21, 1873, they ushered in a brand-new type of grand larceny: robbery of a moving train. The gang loosened a rail at the Turkey Creek cut southwest of town, and when the eastbound locomotive approached, they pulled the rail free using a rope. The engine ran off the tracks and tipped over onto its side, followed by the tender and two baggage cars. The train's engineer, John Rafferty, was crushed in the rollover.

Jesse James thought the train would be carrying $75,000 in gold bullion, but it turned out to only have $2,300 in cash aboard. He had missed the money train by 12 hours. To supplement their meager take, the thieves robbed the passengers of another $1,000. Twenty-eight children of the Chinese aristocracy and their two chaperones were riding the unlucky train that day; they returned home safely but would, from that point on, always refer to America as "Hell Country."

Contrary to popular myths, the CRI&P locomotive was not destroyed and buried at the site. The railroad fixed it up and put it back into service. The large iron wheel used for the roadside marker (erected in 1954) is in no way connected to the infamous event.

Derailment Site, Rte. G30, Adair, IA 50002

No phone

Hours: Always visible

Cost: Free

Directions: Look for the train wheel marker 1.5 miles southwest of Exit 75 (I-75) on Rte. G30.

JESSE JAMES IN IOWA

Jesse James's gang robbed the Ocobock Brothers' Bank (Washington and Jackson Streets) in Corydon on June 3, 1871, netting $6,000. Most of the town was attending Sunday services at the local Methodist church, and was slow to arrange a posse. The bank's looted safe can be seen today at the Prairie Trails Museum of Wayne County (515 E. Jefferson Street, (641) 872-2211, www.prairietrailsmuseum.org) in Corydon. The town doesn't seem to bear any ill will toward the outlaws and celebrates Jesse James Days on the first Saturday in June each year. A new bank now stands on the site of the old bank.

For those of you with a metal detector and plenty of free time, James's gang was also believed to have buried $35,000 in gold coins north of Weston on Route 191. It has never been unearthed.

Algona
The Nazis and Baby Jesus

During World War II, a large POW camp was located at Algona; it held 3,200 captured German soldiers. With plenty of time on their hands, some of the prisoners decided to put it to good use. A group led by Sergeant Eduard Kaib began building a nativity scene in the fall of 1944. It wasn't a common crèche, but a 60-character, half-scale re-creation of the manger scene on December 25, 0 B.C.

The nativity took a year to construct. Of course it had Jesus, Mary, Joseph, and the wise men, but it also had a flock of 30 sheep, a miniature Bethlehem in the distance, and a stream that flowed into a small lake. The men paid for the cement and plaster with their own funds, and erected the nativity near the prison fence so that local folks could peer through the barbed wire at the peaceful scene. (It was Christmas 1945, and even though the war was over, the men were still locked up.)

Whether or not it was their intention, it was a brilliant public relations move. Algonans loved it—so much so that when the Germans were released in 1946, the town asked them if could keep the nativity. The prisoners agreed, on the conditions that it never be resold and that it always be displayed free of charge. It has been erected by the Methodist Men's Club every holiday season since. A permanent display hall was eventually built for it at the fairgrounds, which is where you can see it today.

Kossuth County Fairgrounds, Fair St., Algona, IA 50511

Contact: Methodist Men's Club, First United Methodist Church, 201 E. Nebraska St., Algona, IA 50511

(515) 295-7241 or (515) 295-7242

Hours: December, daily 2–9 P.M.; January–November, by appointment

Cost: Free

www.pwcamp.algona.org/nativity_scene/nativity_scene.htm

Directions: Rte. 169 south, then right on E. Fair St. to the west end of the fairgrounds.

ALTON
Reverend **Robert "Crystal Cathedral" Schuller** was born in Alton in 1926.

Behold the mighty Cheeto in all its gargantuan glory!
Photo by author, courtesy of Tom Straub and Sister Sarah's.

World's Largest Cheeto

When Navy Petty Officer Mike Evans, recently stationed at Pearl Harbor, bought a bag of Cheetos for his three-year-old son, he never expected it would make him a celebrity. Inside the bag was a four-inch, 6/10-ounce, bright orange, edible glob with a five-inch waistline. Evans declared it to be the World's Largest Cheeto! Since the *Guinness Book of World Records* had no such established category (yet), Evans could not be refuted. He put the super-sized snack up for sale on eBay, and the bids started rolling in. Algona disc jockey Bryce Wilson (KGLA-FM) gathered $180 from local boosters to purchase the oddity with the intention of making it a tourist attraction, but he was soon outbid. When the auction reached $1+ million, eBay suspended bidding—the joke had gotten out of hand.

A frustrated Evans decided to donate his delicious discovery to the Algona crowd, but asked them to give the $180 they'd raised to a local food bank. Frito-Lay, who'd heard about the auction, kicked in another $1,000 for the charity.

The World's Largest Cheeto has been left in its original, unnatural state, according to its caretaker and curator Tom Straub, who scrapped his earlier plans to shellac the megamorsel. Straub is the owner of Sister Sarah's bar and restaurant where the Cheeto rests today atop a purple velvet pillow on an orange blown-glass pedestal, protected by a Plexiglas shield, of course. You may stop by to admire it during regular business hours.

Sister Sarah's Bar, 1515 N. McCoy St., PO Box 684, Algona, IA 50511

(515) 295-7757

Hours: Tuesday–Saturday 11 A.M.–Midnight

Cost: Meals $5–$15

Directions: On Rte. 18, a half-mile east of Rte. 169.

OTHER LARGE, UNNATURAL FOODS

The best part about the World's Largest Cheeto is that it's still around for folks to marvel at. Sadly, this isn't the case with a couple of Iowa's other jumbo snacks.

★ The Rice Krispie Treat was invented for Kellogg's in the 1930s by Mildred Day, a graduate of Iowa State's home economics program. In her honor, the **World's Largest Rice Krispie Treat** was built on April 20, 2001, for the university's VEISHEA celebration. It took workers eight hours to convert 820 pounds of Rice Krispies, 220 pounds of butter, and 1,460 pounds of marshmallows into this titanic Treat. After being towed through campus on a float, it was carved up and sold for $1 a bar to raise funds for a local shelter.

★ The folks of Sac County—the Popcorn Capital of the World—built the **World's Largest Popcorn Ball** in 1995. Their creation measured 22 feet in circumference and weighed one ton. (Cracker Jack buys 20 million pounds of popcorn from this region every year.)

★ The **World's Largest Ice Cream Sandwich** was assembled in Dubuque on February 27, 1998. The 2,460-pound treat was made by HyVee employees using Blue Bunny ice cream (see page 37) and two very large cookies from the Metz Baking Company.

Ames
Insect Zoo

The Insect Zoo is not for the squeamish. Hundreds of creepy crawlies are housed in this Iowa State University facility, from grasshoppers and millipedes to hissing cockroaches and blister beetles. They've even got a nice sampling of mosquitoes, ticks, and lice. Best of all, your enthusiastic tour guide will gladly pull out the bugs so you can get a closer look.

If your flesh is crawling just *thinking* about the menagerie, perhaps a better way to view the collection is from a safe distance . . . via the zoo's live webcam. You can control the camera's point of view and can zoom in and out on whatever you want, all from the safety of your own home.

The Insect Zoo is not open for folks to drop in unannounced. You must arrange a tour ahead of time. The one exception to the rule is in September when the Department of Entomology hosts the Insect Horror Film Festival. Students will screen a 1950s *The-Cicada-That-Ate-Des-Moines*-type of film with a science-based discussion before the show. They'll trot out the insects that inspired the flick and will assure you that they'd never, *ever*, let these critters near any toxic waste or radioactive material that might cause them to grow to enormous size.

Promise.

Cross their bug-loving hearts. . . .

Department of Entomology, Science II Building, Room 407, Ames, IA 50011

(515) 294-4537

E-mail: insectzoo@iastate.edu

Hours: By appointment

Cost: Fees vary depending on type of visit

www.ent.iastate.edu/zoo/

Directions: On campus on the south side of Pammel Dr., one block west of Stange Rd.

Insect Horror Film Festival

(515) 294-7400

www.ent.iastate.edu/entclub/horror/

AMES

Two ISU students spotted an orange UFO hovering over Route 69 near Ames on November 11, 1997.

World's First Digital Electronic Computer

In the late 1930s John Vincent Atanasoff had an idea for an electronic computing device, and he needed some help to build it. He hired a graduate assistant named Clifford Berry, who turned out to be a brilliant mathematician in his own right. Between 1939 and 1942 the pair created what was later called the Atanasoff-Berry Computer, or ABC, in the basement of Iowa State University's physics building. The machine could solve equations with 29 unknowns, with answers up to 15 significant figures. Not bad for a first try.

They didn't have time to celebrate, however: World War II broke out, both inventors enlisted in the service, and neither man nor ISU applied for a patent. Unfortunately, Atanasoff was too nice for his own good and had earlier invited a sneaky turd named John Mauchly to visit him in Ames while the ABC was being developed. The Ursinus College professor went back to Philadelphia and, with the help of the U.S. Army, came out with the Electronic Numerical Integrator and Computer, or ENIAC. He applied for, and received, a patent.

Mauchly was known as the Father of the Computer, at least until 1973. That year saw a decision on a seven-year legal battle between Honeywell and the Sperry Rand Corporation. The judge ruled that Mauchly had derived most of his ideas from Atanasoff and Berry, and invalidated his patent for the ENIAC.

A team of ISU professors have since rebuilt the ABC. They started by making a copy of the ABC's memory drum, the only surviving part of the original device, which they uncovered at the Smithsonian. The remaining parts were assembled with the help of manuscripts, interviews, and photographs. You can see it today in the Durham Center on campus.

Durham Center, Iowa State University, Ames, IA 50011

(515) 294-6136

Hours: Monday–Friday 8 A.M.–9 P.M.

Cost: Free

www.iastate.edu

Directions: On campus, southwest of the Parks Library, southeast of Bissell Rd. and Osborn Dr.

Arnolds Park

Arnolds Park

Go ahead, take your Six Flags theme parks with high-concept rides and ticket prices to match. For my money, nothing beats a classic amusement park, and Arnolds Park is one of the best. Billed as the oldest park west of the Mississippi, Arnolds Park has retained much of its original character. The park opened in 1889 when W. B. Arnold built a Chute the Chute slide that jettisoned riders on toboggan boats out into West Lake Okoboji. Other rides were added over the years, including a Fun House, bumper cars, Tipsy House, Roof Garden ballroom, and, in 1927, the Legend roller coaster.

A 1968 tornado swept away some of the park, so it doesn't have all the rides it once did. But the roller coaster has been refurbished and a new Ferris wheel offers you a nice view of the lake. Better see the park while you still can.

Arnold's Park Amusement Park, Lake Park Dr., Arnolds Park, IA 51331

(800) 599-6995 or (712) 332-2183

E-mail: ap@arnoldspark.com

Hours: Late May–Early September, hours vary; check Web site

Cost: Day Pass (over 48 inches) $16.95, Day Pass (36–48 inches) $12.75, Seniors (62+) $12.75, Day Pass (under 36 inches) Free

www.arnoldspark.com

Directions: On the northwest side of Rte. 71, just south of the bridge over the waterway connecting East and West Lake Okoboji.

For those of you who have been coming to Arnolds Park for years, stop by the Iowa Great Lakes Maritime Museum. They've got remnants of the dismantled rides, including a classic bumper car, curved mirrors, and the robotic, piano-playing clown that greeted Fun House visitors. They've also got a speedboat that sank in West Lake Okoboji, but was recently recovered from the murky depths.

Iowa Great Lakes Maritime Museum, Okoboji Spirit Center, 243 W. Broadway Ave., Arnolds Park, IA 51331

(800) 270-2574 or (712) 332-2107

E-mail: ap@arnoldspark.com

Hours: June–August, Monday–Saturday 9 A.M.–9 P.M., Sunday 10 A.M.–6 P.M.; September–May, Monday–Friday 9 A.M.–5 P.M.

Cost: Free

www.okobojimuseum.org

Directions: Adjacent to the amusement park.

The Spirit Lake Massacre

Thirteen-year-old Abbie Gardner was certainly worth more than two horses, 12 blankets, 70 yards of cloth, two powder kegs, 20 pounds of tobacco, and some ribbons, but Dakota leader Inkpaduta took what he could get. Inkpaduta had captured Gardner and three other women three months earlier during the Spirit Lake Massacre, and knew the locals weren't in a bartering mood.

It all started in 1851 when the Dakota nation made a treaty with settlers entering the area. Inkpaduta saw them as invaders, one of whom had murdered his brother Sidominadota and displayed his severed head on a spike. Inkpaduta's frustration boiled over during the harsh winter of 1857. His breakaway tribe was starving, and he tried to barter for food with the settlers, who refused. On March 8 fighting started and, over the next six days, 33 settlers were killed, including Abbie Gardner's parents and brother Rowland. An unknown number of Dakota were also killed.

The female hostages were taken captive; two were later killed, but Gardner and hostage Mrs. Marble were eventually released in exchange for the goods listed above. Inkpaduta evaded capture, lived to see Custer ambushed at Little Big Horn in 1876, and fled to Canada, where he died in 1881.

After a failed marriage, Abbie Gardner returned to the scene of her family's murder in 1891 and, bless her soul, opened the cabin as a tourist attraction. Visitors paid to hear Gardner recount details of the massacre and her captivity. Gardner was well stocked with postcards and souvenir trinkets for anyone who wanted to bring a piece of the tragedy home. . . . and you can still do so today! The restored cabin still stands beside a granite shaft over the Gardner family's graves. The adjoining mini-museum has two beautiful paintings of the massacre, including the *Sad Fate of Mrs. Thatcher*, who drowned in an icy stream. Some believe Gardner painted the scenes, but nobody knows for sure.

Abbie Gardner State Historic Site, Pillsbury Point, 34 Monument Dr., PO Box 74, Arnolds Park, IA 51331

(712) 332-7248 or (712) 352-2643

E-mail: gardner@iowaone.net

Hours: June–September, Monday–Friday Noon–4 P.M., Saturday–Sunday 9 A.M.–4 P.M.

Cost: Free

www.iowahistory.org/sites/gardner_cabin/gardner_cabin.html

Directions: At the intersection of Miriam Lane and Circle Dr., just west of the amusement park.

Keep your hands where I can see them.

Audubon
Albert, the World's Largest Bull

Travelers beware: you don't want to mess with Albert. No sirree, at 35 feet from hooves to horns, this bodacious bovine is not a critter you'd want on your bad side. Oh, he looks kindly enough, but behind those baby blue eyes is a heart of cold steel. And concrete. Forty-five tons of concrete, to be exact. You see, Albert is a statue. A very big statue.

Albert was the brainchild of the Audubon Jaycees. Local beef producers had been promoting their product every year since 1951 through an effort dubbed Operation T-Bone. The marketing campaign was running out of steam, and it needed a gimmick. So Albert, named after Albert Krause of the First State Bank (now the Audubon State Bank), was constructed in 1963–64 using metal from recycled windmills, lots of concrete, and 65 gallons of paint.

This huge Hereford is 100 percent bull, as is plainly obvious from his 5-foot-high testicles. They're worth mentioning because local sweethearts have developed an interesting way to declare their undying love: they scrawl their names on Albert's low-hanging scrotum. In the fall, it's also common for Audubon's football opponents to repaint Albert's danglers in the days leading up to a big game. Is nothing sacred??!?

Albert the Bull Park, E. Division and Stadium Dr., Audubon, IA 50025

(712) 563-2742

E-mail: aced@metc.net

Hours: Always visible

Cost: Free

www.auduboncounty.com/tourism/attractiondetails.htm#albert

Directions: On the east side of Rte. 71 at the south end of town.

Battle Creek
Battle Hill Museum of Natural History

Dennis Laughlin, founder and director of the Battle Hill Museum of Natural History, gets the same question posed to him all the time: "Where do you get all of these animals?" His Web site clears up any confusion: "Well, Mabel, they don't just walk in here and give themselves up, that's for sure. . . . Not *ONE* animal in our collection was killed specifically for our displays! In fact, *SEVERAL* were!"

No, this is not your typical musty institution. Sure, the science behind the displays is accurate and educational, but the attitude is definitely unstuffy. For example, check out the two vultures mounted above the museum entrance; they've been named Bill and Hillary. It's a running joke that surfaces throughout your tour—bashing liberal Democrats that have somehow wronged Laughlin (though details are sketchy) and/or his Board of Directors, five men who, according to Laughlin, "serve without compensation or intelligence." Don't worry—as long as you're a thick-skinned Democrat or a thin-skinned Republican, you'll be just fine here.

The museum's specimens include 600 stuffed critters, among them a two-headed calf, 300 animal skulls, and 90,000 shells, all crammed into a few small rooms. Some of the critters come from as far away as Africa, though most are from right here in the Hawkeye State. Look for the two moose heads on the walls. The first moose wandered into the state in 1989 from Minnesota and was eventually shot by a poacher; his head is mounted like a trophy. The second belonged to another unfortunate visitor from the north who was struck by a semi truck on an Iowa highway. Laughlin has his skull on display.

Battle Hill Museum of Natural History, Highway 175E, Battle Creek, IA 51006

(712) 365-4414

E-mail: bhmuseum@pionet.net

Hours: First Sunday in June–August, 1–5 P.M., or by appointment

Cost: Free; donations encouraged

http://elwood.pioneer.net/~bhmuseum/

Directions: At the east end of town on Rte. 175E.

Boone
Mamie Doud Eisenhower Birthplace

Calling all Mamie Eisenhower fans (you know who you are)! Here's your chance to see the bed where the former First Lady was born on November 14, 1896. But it's not the only piece of Mamieabilia you'll find here, not by a long shot!

Start with the building itself. This simple home was once located across the street, at 718 Carroll Street, and faced the opposite direction. It was moved in 1979 (and dedicated by Bob Hope) when the adjoining church wanted to expand its parking lot. The birthplace now sits atop a new, very large basement that is crammed with Mamie-entos: a pair of pink gowns (her favorite color), a bronzed baby bootie, a barn painting rendered by the Supreme Allied Commander, and a wooden carving of the First Lady that looks suspiciously like Alfred E. Newman. The Doud family Bible rests on a stand in the parlor, and her 1962 Plymouth Valiant is still parked in the garage beside Ike's fishing boots. It's almost as if she never left. . . .

Yet she did, a lonnnnnnnnnnnnng time ago. In fact, Mamie's family moved to Cedar Rapids before Mamie was even a year old. If she'd had any memory whatsoever of this place, it would have been surprising.

709 Carroll St., PO Box 55, Boone, IA 50036

(515) 432-1896 or (515) 432-3342

Hours: April–May, Tuesday–Sunday 1–5 P.M.; June–October, daily 10 A.M.–5 P.M.

Cost: Adults $4, Kids (6–17) $1

www.booneiowa.com

Directions: Three blocks north of Mamie Eisenhower Ave. (Fourth St.), three blocks west of Story St.

If you hit it, blame the locals.

Brayton
Landmark Tree

Back in 1850 surveyor Humphrey Parker was platting the boundary between Audubon and Cass counties, and he jammed his walking stick into the ground to mark the spot. The walking stick was freshly cut from a cottonwood and, over time, took root in the rich Iowa soil. Several years later it was a healthy, thriving tree.

That was the problem. Iowa is crisscrossed by hundreds of dirt roads running north–south and east–west, marked every mile, and this tree was growing right on the centerline of two of them. (That was one accurate surveyor!) Half the tree grew in one county and half grew in another, and neither county wanted it mucking up the road. However, local folks had grown fond of their unique traffic hazard and petitioned for it to remain. They won.

Today the 100-foot cottonwood still blocks both Akron Road and 710th Street, but nobody seems concerned. Of course, the first time there's an accident somebody will wonder why nobody did anything about it sooner. Now you know.

Akron Rd. and 710th St., Brayton, IA 50042

No phone

Hours: Always visible

Cost: Free

www.auduboncounty.com/tourism/attractiondetails2.htm#tree

Directions: Follow the signs to the Landmark Tree heading east out of Brayton on Rte. F65.

Britt
The Hobo Convention and Museum

They've been coming to Britt since 1896—Hairbreath Harry, Box Car Myrtle, Roadrunner Brown, Scoopshovel Scotty, Lord Open Road, Texas Madman, Steamtrain Maury, Polly Ellen Pep, Blue Moon, Mountain Dew, Frisco Jack, Liberty Justice, Slow Motion Shorty, Fishbones, Minneapolis Jewel, Hardrock Kid, and others—to crown their king and queen. Yes, they're hoboes, and they were homeless when homelessness was cool.

Believe it or not, Britt actually *invited* the convention to town, wooing the annual get-together away from Chicago by offering the hoboes a per diem and a place to stay. On the second Saturday in August each year, hoboes from across the nation descend on Britt to celebrate life on the rails. Attendance is the best when the times are the worst and worse when the times are better. There's a parade, an art show, and plenty of mulligan stew. On the final evening a King and Queen of the Hoboes are coronated in Britt's municipal park. Their crowns are fashioned out of Folgers coffee cans, and each winner sports a long, red cape.

Little did organizers know, when they hosted the first convention, that Iowa's Herbert Hoover (see page 106) would, by the 1930s, make the hobo lifestyle a lot more popular. Well, perhaps *popular* isn't the word—maybe *necessary* is more like it. And if you really want to get technical, most of the guys riding the rails during the Great Depression weren't hoboes, but tramps. A tramp is a hobo of unfortunate circumstances, down on his or her luck, who doesn't work much, whereas a hobo chooses the wandering lifestyle, riding the rails from town to town between odd jobs. And a bum? Well a bum is like a tramp, only drunk. And mean. And dirty.

You'll learn all these distinctions at Britt's new Hobo Museum. They've got walking sticks, patched jackets, and more walking sticks on display, with tributes to some of the biggest names in hoboing. If the museum leaves you wanting more, check out the permanent Hobo Jungle along the Soo Line tracks on the north side of town, or have a drink at J&D's Hob Nob Bar (79 N. Main Avenue, (641) 843-3542), or a bite at the Hobo House Café (72 S. Main Avenue, (641) 843-3840).

Hobo Museum, Chief Theater, 51 S. Main Ave., Britt, IA 50423

Contact: Hobo Foundation, PO Box 413, Britt, IA 50423

(641) 843-9104

E-mail: foundation@hobo.com

Hours: June–August, Monday–Friday 9 A.M.–5 P.M., or by appointment

Cost: Adults $1, Kids $1

www.hobo.com

Directions: Six blocks south of Rte. 18 on Rte. 111 (Main Ave.).

AMES
Inventor **George Washington Carver** was the first African American to enroll at Iowa State University (called Iowa Agricultural College and Model Farm at the time), as well as the first African American graduate student, and the first African American faculty member.

Sure, it's corny . . . *that's the point!*

Coon Rapids
Nikita Khrushchev and the Spinning Ear of Corn

Iowans need not be humble when it comes to agriculture; they certainly know what they're doing. In this spirit one of the state's brightest farmers, Bob Garst of Coon Rapids, decided to share his expertise with none other than Soviet Premier Nikita Khrushchev, and invited the leader to visit. To his surprise, Khrushchev accepted, and on September 23, 1959, the premier toured Garst's farm southeast of town. At a lavish picnic the premier confessed, "The slaves of capitalism live very well, but the slaves of communism also live very well." It was a dramatic gesture on both Garst's and Khrushchev's parts, and helped thaw the Cold War, if only by a few degrees.

Even before hosting this famous event, Garst was known throughout the Midwest for developing hardy strains of hybrid corn. Garst died in 1977, and the Garst Seed Company eventually converted his farm into a resort. It's hard to miss from the highway—just turn north at the 5-foot spinning ear of corn. (There's talk of building the World's Largest Ear of Corn in Coon Rapids—50 feet tall, some say—but the plans have yet to germinate.)

Garst Farms Resorts, 1390 Rte 141, Coon Rapids, IA 50058

(712) 684-2964

E-mail: gresort@pionet.net

Hours: Spinning corn always visible; check Web for tours

Cost: Free

www.farmresort.com

Directions: Rte 141 at Fifth Ave. (Rte. N50), on the south side of town.

LIKE WATCHING CORN GROW

Garst's spinning corn cob can be mesmerizing, but after a few turns it's no more interesting than watching corn grow. Don't believe me? Check out Iowa's Corn Cam: www.iowafarmer.com/corncam/corn.html.

Correctionville
The Driftwood Street Jog

Folks in Iowa are nothing if not orderly. When the region was platted prior to statehood, they decided to make each township a six-mile-square plot. But, due to the curvature of the earth, surveyors couldn't strictly follow lines of longitude and latitude; the southern townships would have ended up larger than the northern townships. So, to make a long (boring) story short, the township boundaries were "reset" every sixty miles heading south. The fact that the boundaries do not align perfectly along the correction lines didn't cause much concern for most folks, except in Correctionville.

Town founders decided to establish their community at the intersection of Rock, Kedron, and Union townships in 1855. Fifth Street was laid out along the east–west correction line, the line that inspired this village's name. Driftwood Street runs north–south through Union township, then makes a quick turn to the west at Fifth before realigning along the border between Kedron and Rock townships.

Had you not known the reason for the jog, you might have driven through Correctionville unaware. Now that you do, aren't you glad?

Driftwood and Fifth Sts., Correctionville, IA 51016

No phone

Hours: Always visible

Cost: Free

Directions: Head south on Rte. 31 (Driftwood St.) to where it hits Fifth St.

That's a lot of bullhead.

Crystal Lake
World's Largest Bullhead

Anyone who's fried up a bullhead knows these bottom feeders aren't the tastiest fish around. They are, however, one of the easiest fish to catch in Iowa. But the folks in Crystal Lake seem to be more interested in the sport of fishing than eating these mud-suckers and have erected a large bullhead on the south shore of the lake. It measures 12 feet from snout to tail and sits atop a stone pedestal. Though most bullheads are brown and yellow, this one is green and yellow. Its "whiskers" are three feet long.

State St., Crystal Lake, IA 50432

No phone

Hours: Always visible

Cost: Free

Directions: At the north end of town, where State St. turns at the lake.

Denison
Donna Reed's Hometown

Teenager Donna Belle Mullenger won a blue ribbon for her biscuits at the Iowa State Fair, but all anyone wants to talk about today is her 1953 Academy Award. Who is this multitalented Ms. Mullenger? None other than Donna Reed, Denison's favorite daughter, born here on January 27, 1921.

Reed left town for California at the age of 16 and enrolled at Los Angeles City College, majoring in secretarial studies. She barely needed the diploma; she signed a contract with MGM two months after graduation. Though she is best known for her role in *It's a Wonderful Life* and television's *The Donna Reed Show* (which ran from 1958 to 1966), she received her Oscar for her supporting role in *From Here to Eternity* playing Alma, a prostitute. You can see her golden statuette at Denison's W. A. McHenry House Museum (1428 First Avenue N, (712) 263-3806).

Donna Reed was extremely active in artistic and political causes later in life. She opposed the Vietnam War through Another Mother for Peace and rallied against nuclear weapons and nuclear power. Following her death in 1986, the folks of Denison established the Donna Reed Foundation for the Performing Arts. Each June the foundation hosts the Donna Reed Festival, which includes workshops on acting, singing, dance, and stagecraft, and culminates in the presentation of college scholarships for budding performers. The foundation is also restoring its headquarters in the former 1914 Germania Opera House (technically the Deutsche Opernhause Gesellschaft von Denison), now the Donna Reed Theater. It will include a Donna Reed Museum and a miniature replica of Bedford Falls.

Donna Reed Foundation for the Performing Arts, 1305 Broadway and Main,
   Denison, IA 51442

(712) 263-3334

E-mail: info@donnareed.org

Hours: Monday–Friday 9 A.M.–4 P.M. and by appointment

Cost: Free

www.donnareed.org

Directions Four blocks north of Rte. 30 (Fourth Ave. S) on Main St.

That's a lot of bull.

Earl Marshall, a Lot of Bull

Earl Marshall was the biggest thing to come out of Denison . . . even bigger than Donna Reed! Of course he had a genetic head start: he was a Black Angus bull. Earl Marshall was the byproduct of 30 years of selective breeding by Denison bigwig W. A. McHenry. The bull he created in 1914 became known as King of All Sires. Today, most of the Angus breeding lines can be traced back to this Denison bovine celebrity.

The Denison Angus Association erected a monument to their favorite sperm doner in 1982. As large as Earl Marshall was in real life, he was nowhere near the size of the statue erected in his honor. It was originally located in Sunset Park, but has since been moved to the Crawford County Fairgrounds.

Crawford County Fairgrounds, Rte. 39 and Ave. C, Denison, IA 51442

No phone

Hours: Always visible

Cost: Free

www.denisonia.com/parks_rec.htm

Directions: One block north of Rte. 59/141 on Rte. 39.

CLARION
A UFO reportedly landed in a Clarion soybean field in July 1973, leaving a burned circle and footpad marks.

CORYDON
Corydon was named Springfield until Judge Seth Anderson gambled away the right to rename the town in a poker game.

CYLINDER
Cylinder was named after a piece of machinery that was found in a local river.

DAKOTA CITY
TV newsman **Harry Reasoner** was born in Dakota City on April 17, 1923.

DENISON
Heckling inmates through the bars of the Denison jail is against the law.

Earling
The Earling Exorcism

The Franciscan Sisters of Earling were not used to being called "whores of Jesus," but then again, they had never met Emma Schmidt. Why was Emma so ornery? If you believe the story, Emma was possessed by the Devil!

For many years Emma had been out of sorts. It all started after her drunkard father cursed her on his deathbed for refusing his incestuous advances. After exhausting all medical solutions, her family turned to the local Catholic church, which recommended Father Theophilus Riesinger for the job. He specialized in exorcisms. Father Theophilus, with the help of Pastor Joseph Singer, conducted the 23-day exorcism at the Franciscan convent in Earling.

Emma was not pleased with the sisters' spartan accommodations: she threw food around, both before and after ingesting it (sometimes 30 times a day), she rearranged the furniture by sheer mind power, and she spouted profanity until the cows came home, day after day after day. Her body and head swelled so much the sisters thought she would explode. Father Theophilus had to peel her off the ceiling after she flew up against it. After he tried to cool her down with holy water, she ordered him, "Away with that [you-know-what]!"

The curious Earling townsfolk were drawn to the weird noises and profanity coming from inside the convent, though they never entered the building. They were no safer outside; Emma's power extended beyond the walls of the convent. A black cloud descended on Father Theophilus's car and forced him into a bridge abutment; only St. Christopher saved him . . . or so Emma claimed. Finally, on September 23, 1928, the demon left her body forever. Emma returned home and led a happy, productive life. Take that, Lucifer!!!

Franciscan Convent, 207 Second St., Earling, IA 51530

No phone

Hours: Always visible, view from street

Cost: Free

Directions: One block north of Rte. 37 (Railway St.), across from St. Joseph's Church.

Elk Horn
Danish Windmill

When you think windmills, you probably think Holland. The folks in Elk Horn would like you to think Denmark as well. To drive home the point, they purchased a 60-foot windmill in Norre Snede, Denmark, and had it shipped to Iowa for this nation's bicentennial. The 1848 structure was reconstructed on the south side of town and is used today as an Iowa Welcome Center. The windmill is still in working order, grinding rye; you can purchase the flour at the gift shop.

For the duplicitous among you, the windmill can also be used to trick your friends. Tell them you're jetting off to Europe, take a few snapshots in front of the old structure, and nobody will be any the wiser.

Danish Windmill Museum and Welcome Center, 4038 Main St., PO Box 245, Elk Horn, IA 51531

(800) 451-7960 or (712) 764-7472

E-mail: windmill@netins.com

Hours: Always visible; Welcome Center, December–May, Monday–Saturday 9 A.M.–5 P.M., Sunday Noon–5 P.M.; June–November, Monday–Saturday 8 A.M.–7 P.M., Sunday 10 A.M.–7 P.M.

Cost: Mill Tour, Adults $2, Kids (12 and under) $1

www.danishwindmill.com

Directions: At the south end of town on Rte. 173 (Main St.).

Why, you may ask, did Elk Horn purchase this old windmill? Because Elk Horn (and neighboring Kimballton, see page 34) were settled by Danes in 1867. You can learn all about America's 360,000 or so Danish immigrants at the town's Danish Immigrant Museum. Here you'll see Victor Borge's first piano, shelves and shelves of traditional cookware, Lego blocks, and the tiny Morning Star Chapel, built in thanks by immigrant Charles Walensky and recently carted over from Waterloo.

Come to Elk Horn on Memorial Day and you can join the Tivoli Fest celebration, or Sankt Hans Aften, on the Saturday after Midsummer's Eve, or visit the weekend after Thanksgiving for Jule Fest. If it's Danish, Elk Horn's got it covered.

Danish Immigrant Museum, 2212 Washington St., PO Box 470, Elk Horn, IA 51531

(800) 759-9192 or (712) 764-7001

E-mail: dksec@metc.net

Hours: May 15–September 15, Monday–Friday 9 A.M.–6 P.M., Saturday 10 A.M.–6 P.M., Sunday Noon–6 P.M.; September 16–May 14, Monday–Friday 9 A.M.–5 P.M., Saturday 10 A.M.–5 P.M., Sunday Noon–5 P.M.

Cost: Adults $5, Kids (6–15) $2

www.dkmuseum.org

Directions: Art the west end of town on Rte. F58 (Washington St.).

Go ahead, kiss it.

Emmetsburg
Blarney Stone

Legend has it that when you kiss the Blarney Stone at the castle in Cork, Ireland, you'll be given the gift of eloquence. Back when Elizabeth I demanded Dermot McCarthy surrender his castle to the throne as a sign of loyalty, McCarthy would always come up with an elaborate explanation as to why it couldn't be turned over just yet. His verbal skills impressed the queen, and the myth was born.

If you can't afford to visit the Emerald Isle to bless your troubled tongue, try Emmetsburg. This Iowa town was founded by Irish immigrants and named for martyred Irish patriot Robert Emmet. In 1962 it was named the sister city of Dublin. Three years later, in March 1965, it convinced its European relative to send a chunk of the lucky castle's rock over to the states. It was mounted in cement in front of the Palo Alto County Courthouse, next to a bronze likeness of Emmet, where today you're welcome to pucker up and take your chances. Come by on St. Patrick's Day and you can share the honor with hundreds of slobbering, drunken revelers.

Palo Alto County Courthouse, 1010 S. Broadway, Emmetsburg, IA 50536

(712) 852-2283

E-mail: eburgchamber@iowaone.net

Hours: Always visible

Cost: Free

www.emmetsburg.com

Directions: On Rte. 4 (Broadway) at Tenth St., two blocks south of the Rte. 18 intersection, in front of the courthouse.

Estherville
The Estherville Meteorite

Geez—watch your head around here! On May 10, 1879, a fairly large meteorite missed this Iowa town by a little over a mile. When considered on the scale of the solar system, that was pretty damn close. The meteorite turned out to be one of the largest ever recovered in North America. Three large chunks, weighing 431, 152, and 101 pounds respectively, made up the bulk of the debris, though there were hundreds of other small fragments. The largest hunk had to be dug out of the hole it had made . . . 14 feet deep. (The site is marked by a plaque on Route 4 north of town.)

Chicago's Field Museum of Natural History purchased the largest piece, and the other two biggies were sold off to other museums. The meteorite didn't leave Estherville entirely; a few of the scraps can still be viewed in the Estherville Public Library.

Estherville Public Library, 613 Central Ave., Estherville, IA 51334

(712) 362-7731

Hours: Monday Noon–8 P.M., Tuesday–Wednesday 10 A.M.–6 P.M., Thursday 10 A.M.–
8 P.M., Friday 10 A.M.–5 P.M., Saturday 10 A.M.–2 P.M.

Cost: Free

Directions: Library on Rte. 9 (Central Ave.) at Sixth St., three blocks west of Rte. 4;
marker 1.5 miles north of town on Rte. 4 (Ninth St.).

Exira
Plow-in-Oak Park

Do you need proof why you should always put your tools away? Frank
Leffingwell was out plowing his field in the 1860s when a band of men
passed his farm, all prepared to enlist in the Union Army. Leffingwell
unhitched his mules, leaned his plow against an oak tree, and joined
the group.

Nobody in Exira ever heard from Leffingwell again, though some
believe he survived the Civil War and headed west, looking for gold.
Whatever happened to him, everyone's clear about the fate of the plow
he left behind. The burr oak grew up and around it until, today, the tree
has almost engulfed the device. The plow is all but obscured, with only
the tip and a handle still visible on the outside. If you don't see it soon,
you'll have to trust the X-rays.

Rte. 71, Exira, IA 50076

(712) 268-2762

Hours: Always visible

Cost: Free

Directions: One mile south of town on Rte. 71.

ESTHERVILLE

The word "blizzard" was first used to describe a snowstorm by editor
O. C. Bates of the Estherville *Northern Vindicator* in 1870.

Forest City
Winnebago Birthing Center

Since 1958 Winnebago Industries of Forest City has been making it possible for thousands of Americans to hit the open road, and to do it in style and comfort. The company started by building travel trailers, but in 1966 introduced their first motor home. Praise be!

Here's your chance to see how these blue-highway behemoths are put together. Twice a day the company offers a 90-minute tour of their 60-acre manufacturing facility, from the saw mill and cabinet shop to the metal stamping line. At the end of the tour you'll see the new Winnebagos run through their Pre-Delivery Audit (called a PDA in the biz) where they're forced to endure their first rainstorms and potholes in a simulated environmental chamber.

Winnebago Industries Visitor's Center, 1316 S. Fourth St., Forest City, IA 50436

(800) 643-4892 or (641) 585-6936

E-mail: wit@winnebagoind.com

Hours: Monday–Friday 8 A.M.–4:30 P.M.; Tours, April–October, Monday–Friday 9 A.M. and 1 P.M.

Cost: Free

www.winnebagoind.com

Directions: Off Rte. 69 at the south end of town.

FORT DODGE

A Fort Dodge prison was labeled a "holiday camp" recreational facility on Iowa's 1999 state highway map.

A law passed in 1907 required that all single residents of Fort Dodge between ages 25 and 45 get married.

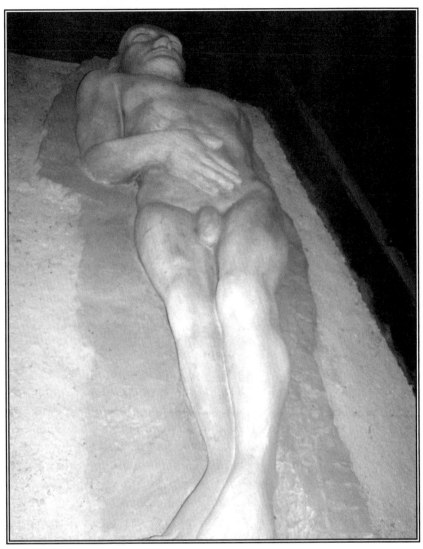

My, what big . . . um . . . *feet* you have.
Photo by author, courtesy of Fort Museum and Frontier Village.

Fort Dodge
A Fake Fake
Be forewarned, the 2,990-pound Cardiff Giant in Fort Dodge's Fort
Museum and Frontier Village is a fake. And since the original Cardiff
Giant was also a fake, this giant is a fake fake.

The story of one of America's greatestest hoaxes started in Ackley, Iowa, in 1866. Cigar maker George Hull was visiting his brother-in-law when he met a traveling Methodist preacher named Reverend Turk. The two got to arguing about whether the Bible was literally true. "Absolutely!" said Reverend Turk, "Every last word." Hull, an atheist, quoted Genesis 6:4, "There were giants in the earth in those days." That too? The preacher never wavered.

A seed had been planted in Hull's mind: he would come up with a hoax to embarrass Reverend Turk and all his fellow believers. In 1868 Hull purchased, for a barrel of lager, a large hunk of gypsum from a Fort Dodge quarry, and had it shipped by rail to Chicago. Over the next three months, two sculptors created a nude, 10-foot-4.5-inch crude likeness of Hull, which he then shipped to the New York farm of his cousin, William "Stub" Newell. The statue was buried behind Newell's barn and left for a year.

On October 16, 1869, Newell hired a work crew to dig him a new well and, using a dowsing rod, specified exactly where they should start digging. Before the end of the day the Cardiff Giant was "discovered." Word spread fast and soon thousands of curiosity seekers (folks like *you*) were flocking to upstate New York to gawk. At 50¢ a head, Newell made a pretty penny. So did Hull, who had a silent, controlling interest in the attraction.

The giant eventually made its way to Syracuse, then Albany, before a Fort Dodge lawyer named Galusha Parsons remembered seeing Hull leaving Iowa two years earlier with a large block of gypsum. On February 15, 1870, the giant's sculptors in Chicago spilled the beans, and Hull, a much richer man, came clean. Interest in the hoax didn't slow much, however, and the giant was moved to New York City and put on display. P. T. Barnum offered to purchase the statue, and when he was rebuffed, he commissioned a new fake. His fake fake attracted more paying customers than the original, probably because he charged half as much to see it.

The Cardiff Giant was eventually sold to a series of private owners, and for many years was in the possession of Des Moines publisher Gardner Cowles Jr., who kept it in his basement rumpus room. The statue currently resides in the Farmer's Museum in Cooperstown, New York. A new fake fake, carved by Cliff Carlson, has been installed at the Fort Museum and Frontier Village in the giant's birthplace: Fort Dodge.

Fort Museum and Frontier Village, S. Kenyon and Museum Rd., PO Box 1798, Fort Dodge, IA 50501

(515) 573-4231

E-mail: thefort@frontiernet.net

Hours: May–October, Monday–Saturday 9 A.M. –5 P.M., Sunday 11 A.M.–5 P.M.

Cost: Adults $6, Kids (6–18) $3

www.fortmuseum.com

Directions: Just east of Rte. 169 on Rte. 20W.

Hanlontown
Sunset on the Railroad Tracks

Life in small-town Iowa can be a little slow—not that there's anything wrong with that. Quite the contrary; the simple life is something to celebrate. For example, the folks in Hanlontown like to honor the sunset. Every June 21 is known as Sundown Day in Hanlontown, a day where everyone comes from miles around to stand on the railroad tracks and admire the setting sun.

Why should this be so amazing? Like the ancient triptychs at Stonehenge, the Rock Island tracks through Hanlontown perfectly mark the summer solstice, aligning directly at the setting sun. Though the railroad didn't lay down the tracks with this in mind, somebody noticed the phenomenon years ago and a local tradition was born. So mark your calendar, grab a lawn chair, and stop on by around dusk.

Sundown Dr., Hanlontown, IA 50444

No phone

Hours: Sunset, June 21

Cost: Free

Directions: One block south of Rte. 9, along the railroad tracks in town.

HARLAN
Iowa's last wild mountain lion was run over by a car near Harlan in August 2001.

HUMBOLDT
Reporter **Harry Reasoner**, who died on August 17, 1991, is buried in Humboldt's Union Cemetery.

A man's mall, skating rink, newspaper office, and ice cream shop is his castle.

Ida Grove
Castles and HMS Bounty

Byron Godbersen loved medieval architecture. A *lot*. This would not even be worth mentioning were he not also filthy rich and willing to put his personal interest on public display. Godbersen was a prolific inventor who founded Midwest Industries, based in Ida Grove. Godbersen contributed funds for most of the major buildings erected in Ida Grove during his lifetime, and on each he left his own special Arthurian mark. The town newspaper's offices, the skate palace, the medical building, the airport, the drugstore, the ice cream shop . . . they all look like castles! Even the golf cart bridge at the country club has a certain Tower of London style.

But that's not all. Godbersen's company developed and manufactures a wide range of "shore–station marine" products, and what better way to demonstrate them to dealers and sales reps than to try them out on a ship? So he had a half-scale reproduction made of HMS *Bounty* and dug an eight-acre lake for it to putt around in. The ship first sailed the waters of Lake La June (named for Godbersen's wife) in April 1970.

Today the *Bounty* is usually in dry dock beside the lake. It's on private property, but it is clearly visible from the road.

Contact: Ida Grove Chamber of Commerce, PO Box 252, Ida Grove, IA 51445

(712) 364-3404

E-mail: igchamber@netllc.net

Hours: Always visible

Cost: Free

http://idagrovechamber.com/castles.html

Directions: All over town, but most are located along Rte. 59.

Jefferson
Ding Dong!

Though the town of Jefferson is the Greene County seat, it's hardly big enough for the downtown to have a skyline. Still, looming 162 feet above the surrounding landscape, the Mahanay Bell Tower makes an impressive silhouette. It was a posthumous gift to the city from William Floyd and Dora Mahanay and was dedicated in 1966. The tower is topped with 14 bronze bells that ring on the quarter hour and play concerts of patriotic songs and religious hymns three times a day.

The Mahanay Bell Tower is large enough that it has an observation deck, which is accessible via elevator. From twelve stories up you can survey the view, which is decidedly flat and crop-covered. In other words: Iowa.

Mahanay Bell Tower, 100 E. Lincoln Way, Jefferson, IA 50129

(515) 386-2155

E-mail: chamber@jeffersoniowa.com

Hours: June–August, daily 11 A.M.–4 P.M.; May and September, Saturday–Sunday 11 A.M.–4 P.M.; Music, 11 A.M., 2 P.M., and 5 P.M.

Cost: Adults $1, Kids (12 and under) 50¢

www.jeffersoniowa.com

Directions: Two blocks east of Rte. 4 (Elm St.) on Rte. E53 (Lincoln Way), on the courthouse square.

JEFFERSON

Pollster **George Gallup** was born at 703 S. Chestnut Street in Jefferson on November 18, 1901.

Ring Ring!

If you think Ma Bell, or her current corporate equivalent, has a stranglehold on the entire United States, think again. Iowa is known for its independent telephone companies, and the Jefferson Telephone Company is still going strong. The town originally had *two* companies—the Cockerill Telephone Company and the Farmers (later Citizens) Mutual Company—which meant folks had to install two phones in their homes to reach everyone in town. The companies merged in 1940, forming the current utility.

The Jefferson Telephone Company collected phones, switchboards, insulators, and cables over the years, and they're all on display in this small basement museum. You'll see hand-cranked units, early dial phones, ultramodern Swinglines, and even a chunk of the first transcontinental toll cable. Best of all, your tour is conducted by a current, well-informed employee of the company—whoever is free in the office when you arrive. The collection also serves as a miniature natural history museum, filled with stuffed dead critters shot or caught by C. H. Daubendiek, one of the company's former owners.

Jefferson Telephone Company Museum, 105 W. Harrison St., Jefferson, IA 50129

(515) 386-4141

Hours: Daily 8:30 A.M.–4:30 P.M.

Cost: Free

http://showcase.netins.net/web/jtco/the_company.htm

Directions: Two blocks east of Rte. 4 (Elm St.), one block south of Rte. E53 (Lincoln Way).

Kimballton
The Little Mermaid

Long before Walt Disney Studios seized the image of the Little Mermaid and copyrighted her, she was an enduring symbol of Danish culture. "The Little Mermaid" was written by Hans Christian Anderson in 1837. A statue of the Little Mermaid was eventually placed on a rock in Copenhagen Harbor.

Today, she's also right here in Kimballton, a thousand miles from any ocean. The sculpture is a small-scale replica of the original; her rock sits in a small fountain in City Park.

For those of you looking for more out of your visit to the area than a second-generation statue, plan on coming to Kimballton on the second full weekend in October for the Iowa State Hand Corn Husking Contest. The town's promotional material promises "Kimballton has a reputation as having one of the most organized, efficient, fair, and accurate contests in the country." As you may know, most hand corn-husking competitions are rigged. But not here.

Little Mermaid Park, Main St., Kimballton, IA 51543

(712) 764-4343

Hours: Always visible

Cost: Free

www.metc.net/audubonco/tourism/attractiondetails.htm

Directions: On Rte. 173 (Main St.), just south of Rte. 44.

Laurens
Fore!

The rules of golf are fairly straightforward, but here's a question you're not likely to run into unless you play the Laurens Golf and Country Club: what if your ball strikes a Cessna while both are in flight? Do you play it where it lies, or can you tee off again? And if you do, will it cost you a stroke? You see, the main fairway at this town's golf course doubles as an airport runway. None of the planes that fly in and out of Laurens are all that big—no Boeing 747s—but they're enough of a hazard that they're worth a mention. Ask at the clubhouse.

Laurens Golf and Country Club, 12582 Highway 10, Laurens, IA 50554

(712) 841-2287

Hours: Always visible

Cost: Free; Green fee extra

Directions: Just west of town on Rte. 10.

The Straight Story

In 1994, 73-year-old Alvin Straight learned that his brother Henry (renamed Lyle for the movie) had suffered a stroke. The pair had been estranged for years, but Alvin decided that there wasn't much time left to make amends. Henry lived in Mount Zion, Wisconsin, 253 miles from Alvin's home in Laurens. Worse still, Alvin was without a driver's license—it had been revoked due to his failing eyesight—and he had to use two canes to walk.

But Alvin Straight had a Rehds riding lawn mower. So he built a trailer, filled it with provisions, hitched it to the Rehds, and headed east out of town. He got as far as West Bend before the mower broke down.

That wasn't enough to stop a stubborn cuss like Straight. Back in Laurens he purchased a used John Deere and took off for Wisconsin again. At five miles per hour it took Straight a while to reach Mount Zion, but he made it. Straight crossed the Mississippi River at Prairie du Chien, but his mower broke down just short of his brother's place. He had to be towed the last few miles.

Alvin Straight's story might have been forgotten had it not been made into a 1999 movie by director David Lynch. Actor Richard Farnsworth portrayed Straight and earned an Oscar nomination for his efforts. (The 1966 John Deere used in the film is on display at the Riegel Blacksmith Shop in Clermont.) Alvin Straight died in 1996, but there is talk of turning his home into a tourist attraction.

Straight Home, 120 Section Line Rd., Laurens, IA 50554

No phone

Hours: always visible

Cost: Free

Directions: On 440th St. (Section Line Rd.), at Third St.

LARRABEE

When 12.99 inches of rain fell on Larrabee on June 24, 1891, it set the Iowa state record for heaviest rainfall in a 24-hour period.

Yummy, yummy, yummy.
Photo by author, courtesy of the Wells Dairy.

Le Mars
Ice Cream Capital of the World

Who makes more ice cream than anyone else in the nation? Nope, not Ben or Jerry, not Baskin or Robbins, but the Wells Dairy in Le Mars, the Ice Cream Capital of the World (a title bestowed by the Iowa legislature in April 1994). Started in 1913 by Fred Wells, this company has grown to the point where 190,000 cows are needed just to keep the Blue Bunny ice cream assembly line churning. The dairy produces more than 100 million gallons each year, including 14 different types of vanilla. Also, if you laid all the Popsicle sticks Wells uses each year end-to-end, they'd stretch 68,377 miles—enough to circle the globe three times! These are just a few of the interesting things you'll learn at the company's visitor center.

If you want to skip the museum and go straight to the goodies, there's a 1920s-style ice cream parlor attached where you can get phosphates, floats, sundaes, and banana splits the way they used to make them: fat-filled and fantastic. If you're a low-carb diet nut and want them to use fat-free yogurt or sugar-free ice cream they'll oblige, but understand, you're flying in the face of ice cream tradition. Ice cream without sugar and cream is, well, ice. Flavored ice. Yuck.

Finally, mark your calendars: July 4 isn't just Independence Day in Le Mars, it's the annual Ice Cream Days Celebration. Be sure to pack those stretch pants.

Ice Cream Capital of the World Visitor Center, 16 Fifth Ave. NW, Le Mars, IA 51031
(712) 546-4090
E-mail: alwatson@bluebunny.com
Hours: April–August, Monday–Saturday 9 A.M.–5 P.M., Sunday 1–5 P.M.;
   September–March, Monday–Friday 11 A.M.–5 P.M., Saturday 9 A.M.–5 P.M., Sunday 1–5 P.M.
Cost: Adults $3, Kids (5–12) $1
www.wellsdairy.com or www.bluebunny.com
Directions: At the intersection of Rte. 75 (Fifth Ave.) and Rte. 3 (Plymouth St.).

LE MARS
The name Le Mars was derived from the wives of six Illinois Central railroad officials in 1870. The women—**L**ucille, **E**lizabeth, **M**ary, **A**nna, **R**ebecca, and **S**arah—had accompanied their husbands to the new town site while the tracks were being laid.

Logan
Museum of Religious Arts

For centuries the world's religious establishments have been the largest patron of the arts, from the Sistine Chapel to the Seated Buddha. That tradition continues to this day at places like the Museum of Religious Arts, a non-denominational (but definitely Christian) institution. The centerpiece of this museum is the King of Kings exhibit: nine full-size dioramas from the life of Christ. These wax sculptures were purchased from Sunken Gardens of St. Petersburg, Florida, when that roadside attraction went bankrupt. Follow the Messiah's life from the Annunciation to the Ascension, and all the high points in between.

They've also got a collection of dolls dressed in nun habits of various orders, a replica of a southwestern mission chapel, stained glass windows depicting the Bible's eight virtues, films and videos of the Holy Land, and an extensive research library.

2697 Niagara Tr., Logan, IA 51546

(712) 644-3888

E-mail: museum@loganet.net

Hours: November–March, Tuesday–Saturday 9 A.M.–5 P.M., Sunday Noon–5 P.M.;
  April–October, Monday–Saturday 9 A.M.–5 P.M., Sunday Noon–5 P.M.

Cost: Adults $5, Kids (5–12) $3

www.mrarts.org

Directions: South of town on Rte. 30, then west on Niagara Tr.

MANSON
A 24-mile-wide crater, centered around present-day Manson, was left by an enormous meteorite 74 million years ago. There is little visible evidence of the crater still left.

MOVILLE
A Moville postal employee refused to "deliver sin" to people on his route in 1994. The problem? *Newsweek's* cover story about lesbians, which showed a same-sex couple on its cover.

Friendly, yes . . . unless you're a duck!

Mallard
Big Mallard

Perched atop a sign on the outskirts of Mallard is the largest duck you've
ever seen, at least in these parts, perhaps anywhere. The sign proclaims,
"Welcome to Mallard: We're Friendly Ducks."

Oh, really? You wouldn't say that if you were a duck.

Mallard was named by railroad owner Charles Whitehead. If the man loved anything, it was hunting, and his favorite quarry were plover, curlew, and mallards. He even decided to name towns after them, all in a row. Curlew is the first town northwest of Mallard; Plover is the first town to the southeast. Neither of these little burgs has tried to curry favor with their local bird populations by building a statue in their honor. Mallard has, and don't think the ducks are fooled.

Rte. 4, Mallard, IA 50562

No phone

Hours: Always visible

Cost: Free

Directions: At the corner of 460th Ave. (Rte. 4) and 490th St. (Rte. B63).

Moingona and Boone
Kate Shelley, Train Saver

We should all be as brave as 15-year-old Kate Shelley . . . let's just hope we never have to be. On July 6, 1881, a torrential rainfall weakened the Honey Creek train trestle near her family's farm. This was confirmed when a lone locomotive, dispatched to check the track, plunged into the still-raging creek; two of its four crew drowned and the others were stranded in trees.

Shelley heard it all from her home. She knew an eastbound Chicago-Northwestern passenger train would soon meet its doom if she didn't warn the Moingona station agent, so she did the only thing she could do: she followed the tracks back toward the station, which meant she had to crawl across the 696-foot Des Moines River railroad bridge. At night. During the thunderstorm. Toward the oncoming train.

Still, she made it. The railroad was understandably thankful, and issued her a golden watch, $100 cash, and a lifetime railroad pass. Though she later studied to be teacher, Shelley returned to Moingona in 1903 to accept the position of station manager. Two years earlier a new bridge had been built north of town, and was named the Kate Shelley High Bridge. It's the longest double-track train trestle in the world at 2,685 feet, and soars 185 feet over the valley below. Shelley never got the chance to crawl across this one; she died of tuberculosis in 1912.

Kate Shelley High Bridge, 200th St., Moingona, IA 50036

No phone

Hours: Always visible

Cost: Free

www.booneiowa.com

Directions: Head north out of Boone on Marion St., then left on 198th Rd. Follow 198th Rd. until 200th St. turns to the right; drive west on 200th St. and look to your left.

Today a museum is located in the old Moingona station. You can watch a film about Shelley's courageous feat in a theater made from a converted Rock Island passenger coach, which is parked adjacent to the museum on a set of abandoned tracks. If you hike a short distance to the south, you'll see the crumbling abutments from the former Des Moines River bridge.

Kate Shelley Park and Railroad Museum, 1198 232nd St., Moingona, IA 50036

(515) 432-1907

Hours: June–September, Saturday–Sundays 1–5 P.M., or by appointment

Cost: Free

http://homepages.opencomnc.com/bchs/BCHSKateShelleyRailroadMuseum.htm

Directions: Head south on R18 from Rte. 30, turn left on Moingona Rd., then left on 232nd St. to McCall Rd.

NORTH SIOUX CITY

In August 1997, a family in North Sioux City reported that a UFO followed their vehicle eastward through Stone State Park, where a pack of hyenas jumped their car. Later, ghostlike "angels" appeared at their home near the foot of their father's bed, while the man's sister had dreams of "frog men." His nephew found unexplained puncture wounds on one pinkie and one little toe.

Crawl across THAT!

Do you still have trains on the brain? Chug on over to Boone where you can ride a passenger coach pulled by the last commercially produced steam-powered locomotive ever built: Engine Number 8419 from China's Datong Locomotive Works. It was built in 1989 and purchased for $355,000 by this museum. Once a day, and twice on weekends, the Boone & Scenic Valley Railroad makes the round-trip to Fraser and back, passing over the Bass Point Creek High Bridge (but not the Kate Shelley High Bridge). In September each year Boone celebrates train-themed Pufferbilly Days.

Boone & Scenic Valley Railroad, Iowa Railroad Historical Society, 225 Tenth St., PO Box 603, Boone, IA 50036

(800) 626-0319 or (515) 432-4249

E-mail: b&svrr@tdsi.net

Hours: Train, June–October, Monday–Friday 1:30, Saturday–Sunday (Steam) 11 A.M., 1:30
and 4 P.M.; Museum, Monday–Friday 9 A.M.–4 P.M., Saturday–Sunday 10 A.M.–6 P.M.

Cost: Coach, Adults $14, Kids (3–12) $5; Valley View Car, Adults $18, Kids (3–12) $7;
Caboose, Adults $20, Kids (3–12) $10; Dessert train $25; Dinner train, $50

www.scenic-valleyrr.com

Directions: Just east of Division St. on Tenth St., seven blocks east of Story St. and six
blocks north of Mamie Eisenhower St. (Fourth St.).

Onawa
Birthplace of the Eskimo Pie

Christian K. Nelson was running an ice cream shop in Onawa in 1920
when a demanding child, who had only a nickel, asked for a candy bar
and an ice cream cone. Nelson wasn't able to accommodate the brat, but
the request got him working on a prototype of a chocolate-dipped con-
coction he later dubbed the I-Scream Bar.

Nelson took his invention to an Omaha confectioner who passed
on a partnership, though one of the candymaker's employees, Russell
Stover, jumped at the prospect. By 1922 the pair had a patent, a new
brand name—Eskimo Pie—and more than a million orders a year.
Nelson eventually bought out Stover's interest in the operation, then
retired at the ripe old age of 35. Today Onawa honors its place in ice
cream history with an exhibit on Nelson at the local historical museum.

Monona County Historical Museum, 47 Twelfth St., Onawa, IA 51040

(712) 423-2776 or (712) 423-2867

E-mail: gmaginny@longlines.com

Hours: June–August, Saturday–Sunday 1–4:30 P.M., or by appointment

Cost: Free

Directions: Two blocks west of Rte. K45 (Tenth St.), two blocks south of Rte. K42
(220th St.).

ONAWA

Onawa's Iowa Avenue is the widest main street in the United States.

Walt Disney, take me away!

Pocahontas
World's Largest Pocahontas

For many years the town of Pocahontas was Pocahontasless. That all changed in 1954 when Albert and Frank Shaw constructed a 25-foot-tall concrete Indian maiden on the east side of town. Pokie, as she's called by locals, gestures tourists to a now-closed gift shop with a tipi-shaped facade.

Though she gets a fresh coat of paint now and then, things don't look good for Pokie. Will she fall victim to civic indifference from the folks of "The Princess City"? Let's hope not.

Elm Ave. and Sixth St., Pocahontas, IA 50574

(712) 335-3935

E-mail: pcedc@evertek.net

Hours: Always visible

Cost: Free

www.pocahontasiowa.com

Directions: At the east end of town on Rte. 3 (Elm Ave.), across from the cemetery.

Rock Rapids
Bridge to Nowhere

Observant visitors to the Melan Bridge in Rock Rapids will quickly notice one thing: it goes nowhere. It doesn't cross a river, or railroad tracks, or another highway. Some bridge.

Some bridge, indeed. Built in 1894 over the Rock River, the Melan Bridge was the world's first reinforced concrete bridge. The revolutionary method was patented by Austrian engineer Josef Melan. Though it might not look like anything special today, it certainly was at the time. That's why, when the Melan Bridge began showing signs of wear from years of traffic, it was moved to its own park on the east side of town.

It is safe to say that had the Melan Bridge never been built, your trip to this secluded corner of the state would have been much more difficult. Count the concrete bridges you cross on your trip and you'll see what I mean. Most bridges today are made from reinforced concrete— it's durable and inexpensive—and the idea started right here in Rock Rapids.

Emma Stater Park, Second Ave., Rock Rapids, IA 51246

No phone

Hours: Always visible

Cost: Free

Directions: At the east end of town on Rte. 9 (Second Ave.), adjacent to the water tower.

SIOUX CITY

Jerry "The Beaver" Mathers was born in Sioux City on June 2, 1948, but he did *not* die in Vietnam. The family moved to California when Jerry was two years old.

Sioux City
The Crash of United Flight 232

On July 19, 1989, United Flight 232 was en route from Denver to Chicago when the passengers and crew heard a loud explosion in the tail section. Pilot Al Haynes quickly realized the DC-10's Number 2 engine had malfunctioned, cutting off virtually all of the plane's hydraulic power. The hydraulic lines had been severed by shards of the engine's fan blades as they disintegrated. (Part of the rear engine was eventually found near Alta.) But by thrusting the plane's two wing engines, which were controlled through manual lines located in the floor by off-duty captain Dennis Fitch (who just happened to be on the flight), Haynes and his crew were able to limp the airliner back to Sioux City.

The DC-10 stayed aloft for 44 more minutes, allowing airport response teams to move into position. As the airliner approached Runway 22, its right wing dipped, gouging an 18-foot-long trench in the concrete before it ripped off. The plane broke into three main pieces and skidded to a stop in a cornfield. Of the 284 passengers and 12 crew aboard, 112 died, all passengers. Considering what could have happened, it was remarkable that anyone made it out alive.

One of the most enduring images of that day, a photo of Colonel Dennis Nielsen of the Iowa National Guard carrying a child away from the wreck, was made into a memorial sculpture along the Missouri River downtown, just west of the Anderson Dance Pavilion (100 Larsen Park Road). The crash was the basis for the 1993 movie *Fearless*.

Sioux Gateway Airport, 6715 Harbor Dr., Sioux City, IA 51111

(712) 279-6165

Hours: Always visible

Cost: Free

www.flysiouxgateway.com

Directions: Head west three blocks on Ogden Ave. (Rte. 378) from I-29, on the south side of town.

SIOUX CITY

A cigar-shaped UFO that "flew sideways" was spotted just west of the Sioux City airport by a Mid-Continent Airline pilot in January 1951.

Eppie and Popo

Few women have had as much influence on the twentieth-century American mind as Eppie and Popo Friedman. Never heard of them? Yes you have, but you probably know them as Ann Landers and Abigail "Dear Abby" Van Buren.

Identical twins Esther Pauline "Eppie" and Pauline Esther "Popo" Friedman were born in Sioux City on July 4, 1918, to Abe and Becky Friedman. Their parents had emigrated from Russia ten years earlier. Abe sold chickens from a pushcart at first, but eventually opened a grocery. By the time the twins were in school he owned three theaters downtown: the Orpheum, the Capitol, and the Hippodrome. The Friedman household hosted a continual stream of vaudeville performers whom the twins plied for personal advice and juicy stories of the sin-filled world outside Iowa.

Eppie and Popo attended North Central Junior High and later Central High. At Central High they started offering advice to their wide-eyed classmates during lunch, mostly by repeating the bawdy sex tales they'd heard from the chorus girls.

The twins graduated in 1936 and enrolled at Morningside College where they were remembered for their matching skunk-fur coats. They cowrote a column for the *Collegian Reporter* titled "Campus Rats," and rat they did. Students claimed the dirt-dishing column was the most popular feature in the paper. It included a weekly rundown of Morningside scandals, such as who got drunk at the football team's after-game party, or who attended *Fields of Alicia*, a cinematic tour of a nudist colony which was being shown at their father's "art house" Capitol Theater.

While in college, Eppie and Popo both became engaged; Eppie to Mort Phillips and Eppie to Jules Lederer. As was their style, they married in a joint ceremony at Shaare Zion Synagogue on July 2, 1939. The reception was held at the Martin Hotel. Marriage, job opportunities, and World War II finally separated the nearly conjoined sisters and led them away from Sioux City for good.

Freidman Home, 1722 Jackson St., Sioux City, IA 51105

Private phone

Hours: Private property, view from street

Cost: Free

Directions: One block east of Nebraska St., three blocks north of 14th St.

Trinity Heights

If you really want to impress God, think BIG! That's what the folks of Queen of Peace did in Sioux City, and look at them now: they've got a 30-foot stainless steel Virgin Mary and a new 33-foot Jesus. (Technically, the statues are called the Immaculate Heart of Mary Queen of Peace and the Sacred Heart of Jesus, but you'll learn all about that on your visit.)

Back in 1991, when this 53-acre hilltop shrine was just an idea, folks from the Queen of Peace were on the site praying as United Flight 232 crashed on the other side of town (see page 47). The faithful took the relatively low loss of life as a sign that their holy mission was blessed. When the Mega-Mary arrived a year later, their beliefs were validated. Jesus was then erected in 1998.

Another miracle arrived in the form of a 22-foot-long, life-sized sculpture of da Vinci's *Last Supper*, carved by Jerry Traufler of nearby Le Mars. It took Traufler seven years to complete, and he was assisted by thirteen men in his community who posed as Jesus and the 12 apostles.

Future plans for Trinity Heights include a Way of the Saints, a four-shrine pathway lined with 60 statues of holy men and women, and a retirement village.

33rd St. and Floyd Blvd., PO Box 1707, Sioux City, IA 51102

(712) 239-8670

E-mail: trinityheights@aol.com

Hours: April–September, daily 10 A.M.–9 P.M.; October–March 10 A.M.–4 P.M.

Cost: Free

www.sctrinityheights.org

Directions: Head south on Floyd Blvd. from Rte. 75 to 33rd St.

SIOUX CITY

Fred "Gopher" Grandy was born in Sioux City on June 29, 1948. He went on to represent Iowa's Sixth (today's Fifth) congressional district from 1987 to 1995. Grandy became interested in politics when he was the teenage roommate of David Eisenhower at Phillips Exeter Academy. Grandy would later serve as best man at Eisenhower's marriage to Julie Nixon.

Unlucky Sergeant Floyd

Poor Sergeant Charles Floyd. This member of Lewis and Clark's Corps of Discovery expedition expired on August 20, 1804, from what was likely a ruptured appendix. It was only three months into the Corps's journey, and it probably generated some anxiety among the rest of the party. But as luck would have it, Floyd was the only member of the original crew to die on the three-year cross-country trip. (Floyd has the unique distinction of being the first U.S. soldier to die west of the Mississippi River.)

Lewis and Clark buried Floyd on August 21 on a bluff where Sioux City stands today. Floyd's grave slid down the hill in 1857, but locals found his bones and replanted him atop the hill, but a little farther back. His body was unearthed in 1900 and a casting was made of his skull for future reference. A 100-foot obelisk monument was erected on the spot in 1901, which in 1960 was named a National Historic Landmark, the first ever designated.

Floyd's Bluff, 2601 S. Lewis Blvd., Sioux City, IA 51101

No phone

E-mail: scpm@sioux-city.org

Hours: Daylight hours

Cost: Free

www.lewisandclarktrail.com and www.cr.nps.gov/nr/travel/lewisandclark/ser.htm

Directions: South of town at Glenn Ave. and Lewis Blvd. (Rte. 75), north of Rte. 20.

The casting of Floyd's noggin came in handy years later when Sioux City folks opened the Sergeant Floyd River Museum & Welcome Center. Forensic scientists used it as a reference for the statue of the sergeant that now resides inside this welcome center/survey boat along the riverfront.

Sergeant Floyd River Museum & Welcome Center, 1000 Larsen Park Rd., Sioux City, IA 51103

(712) 279-0198

E-mail: scpm@sioux-city.org

Hours: Daily 9 A.M.–5 P.M.

Cost: Free

www.sioux-city.org/museum

Directions: Heading south on Dakota Ave., follow the signs to the Argosy Casino, then drive west on Larsen Park Rd. until you see the boat on the left.

If you want to see a spooky re-enactment of Sergeant Floyd's burial, head over to the new Lewis & Clark Interpretive Center, where two lifelike Lewis and Clark robots plant their unfortunate underling on the bluff. Floyd, in the pine coffin, is not as animated. Elsewhere in the museum, an animatronic Seaman, the Newfoundland dog who came along on the expedition, keeps a watchful eye on a caged prairie dog robot.

Lewis & Clark Interpretive Center, 900 Larsen Park Rd., Sioux City, IA 51103

(712) 224-5242

E-mail: ahansen@siouxcitylcic.com

Hours: June–September, daily 9 A.M.–6 P.M.; October–May, Tuesday–Saturday 9 A.M.– 5 P.M., Sunday 1–5 P.M.

Cost: Free

www.siouxcitylcic.com

Directions: Heading south on Dakota Ave., follow the signs to the Argosy Casino, then drive west on Larsen Park Rd. as it passes under the bridge until you see the statues on the left.

Witch Hunt

If you think that witch hunts were something that happened long ago in places like Salem, Massachusetts, perhaps you should learn about what happened in Sioux City in the mid-1950s. It all began on August 31, 1954, when eight-year-old Jimmy Bremmers disappeared from the front of his home at 2701 Cottage Avenue. Suspicion immediately fell on door-to-door salesman Ernest Triplett, a lifelong drifter and acknowledged simpleton who had been working in the neighborhood that night. Triplett had moved to Sioux City three weeks prior to Bremmers's disappearance; he worked on commission selling music lessons for the Flood Music Company (410 Fourth Street, (712) 255-0751) and was living downtown at the Bus Hotel (Fourth and Douglas streets, since demolished).

Triplett was packed off to the Mental Health Institute at Cherokee, a hospital staffed mostly by foreign-trained doctors who had not yet gotten their U.S. licenses. When Bremmers's body was discovered on September 29 along Ridge Road just outside the city and county limits, law enforcement brought Triplett to the site, where he acted suspiciously.

But there was a reason for his odd behavior, and it had nothing to do with the murder: Triplett had been "medicated" with speed, barbiturates, and 500 milligrams of LSD by his attending physician at Cherokee, Dr. Anthony Sainz. Investigators soon announced that they'd obtained a confession from their suspect.

Triplett was tried in Le Mars, the Plymouth County seat (where the body was found). Much of the defense's testimony focused on his alibi; Triplett claimed he was back at the Bus Hotel listening to *The Liberace Show*. The prosecution used it against him. A juror later explained, "[The prosecution] had a very weak case against Triplett, but he admitted in open court that he listened to Liberace on the radio, and a man who does that is liable to do anything." Yikes. The jury found Triplett guilty of second-degree murder, and he was packed off to the Fort Madison penitentiary.

End of story? Not by a long shot.

Triplett was behind bars, yet Sioux City was rocked by another murder on July 10, 1955. Twenty-two-month-old Donna Sue Davis was snatched from her crib in a home on Isabella Street (between Villa Avenue and W. 14th Street) and found dead in a cornfield between South Sioux City and Dakota City, Nebraska. Detectives were baffled, so they tried the *Casablanca* strategy: round up the usual suspects.

While there were no usual suspects, police were armed with Iowa's new "sexual psychopath" statute, passed five months earlier in the wake of the Bremmers murder. According to the law, anyone whom authorities believed had a "propensity" for sexual violence could be locked up in a state psychiatric facility. Ward 15 East at the Mental Health Institute for the Insane and Inebriates at Mount Pleasant had been established for just such "psychopaths," and it had 25 empty beds.

But not for long. Police took it upon themselves to define a "sexual psychopath" as anyone outside the mainstream sexual norm, including homosexuals or anyone in possession of pornography. Sioux City police trolled for gays at the bar in the Warrior Hotel, a popular hangout for the city's almost invisible gay community. They nabbed twenty men in September 1955 and packed them off to Mount Pleasant, and nobody did much of anything to stop it. After seven months in the mental hospital, most were released as "cured." To their credit, many of the doctors at

Mount Pleasant soon discovered there was nothing wrong with the patients assigned to them, and actively worked to secure their release. By then, however, the men's personal lives were in tatters, and most left Iowa forever.

And what ever happened to Triplett? His conviction was overturned in 1972 when the case was reviewed on appeal. It was the first time anyone learned that Dr. Sainz had drugged the suspect, putting his confession in serious doubt. In fact, complete transcripts of the confession showed that Triplett had no real knowledge of *any* of the particulars surrounding the murder. In fact, police noted that he was barely awake during the interrogation, and had been coerced into signing the document that sent him away for almost twenty years. Since there was no physical evidence whatsoever linking him to the case, he was released. The entire sad story is told in detail in Neil Miller's fascinating book *Sex-Crime Panic.*

Warrior Hotel (closed), Sixth and Nebraska Sts., Sioux City, IA 51101

No phone

Hours: Always visible

Cost: Free

Directions: Three blocks east of Pearl St., five blocks north of I-29, downtown.

Stanhope
Teeny-Weeny Town

First, a warning: the Country Relics Village is in danger of becoming just that, a relic. After more than 20 years, owners Varlen and Fern Carlson are thinking of retiring, and have not yet found a buyer for their unique collection. Before you put this destination on your itinerary, you might want to give them a call first.

The whole thing started in 1979 when the Carlsons moved the 1882 Stanhope Depot to their farm north of town. They planned to restore it in time for the town's 1983 Centennial, and in the process became infected with the Building Bug. Today they have a farm machinery dealership, a schoolhouse, a chapel, a livery stable, an outhouse, a blacksmith shop, a general store, a chicken coop, and so on, and they're all filled with spooky department store mannequins—120 dummies in all! The buildings, some purchased and some constructed on a half-scale model, are crammed with every sort of rural artifact imaginable, from dry goods to sewing machines and kids' pedal tractors to a working 1923 Model T Ford. And the entire complex is overrun with free roaming barn cats.

If it all seems like too much to absorb, stop by the Century Hall of Miniatures, where you can view a 1/12-scale replica of the Living History Horse Farm in Des Moines, as well as a few doll houses, all in one convenient location.

Country Relics Village, Rte. 17 N, Stanhope, IA 50246

(515) 826-4FUN

E-mail: ctryrcs@netins.net

Hours: May–October, Monday–Saturday 10 A.M.–5 P.M., Sunday 12:30 P.M.–5 P.M.

Cost: Adults $5, Kids $2

www.countryrelicsvillage.com

Directions: One and a half miles north of town on Rte. 17.

SOLDIER
Soldier was named for a dead body, dressed in a uniform, discovered along the river.

SPENCER
Spencer law prohibits a person from making personal remarks to strangers.

Most of Spencer's business district burned to the ground on June 27, 1931, after a youngster ignited a box of fireworks with a misplaced sparkler.

Storm Lake
Living Heritage Tree Museum

Just as Joni Mitchell predicted, somebody has taken all the trees and put them in a tree museum . . . but no, they didn't pave Paradise in the process. The trees in this museum are planted outside, where they belong.

So why are these trees so special? They've been propagated from famous trees planted at historic sites around the world. They've got the original Delicious apple (see page 125), but that one, while undoubtedly groundbreaking, can't even compare to the nearby Isaac Newton apple, which, according to legend, dropped a fruit to inspire Newton's theory of gravity. There's also a Johnny Appleseed apple and an American sycamore grown from seeds brought to the moon aboard *Apollo 14*. These trees make lesser saplings, such as the Wright Brothers walnut, the Colonel Sanders ash, the Buffalo Bill cottonwood, the Bunker Hill oak, the Lindbergh crab apple, the Henry Clay ginkgo, the Alex Hale silver maple, and the George Washington walnut (not cherry!) seem like B-list trees in comparison.

Sunset Park, Lakeshore Dr. and Ontario St., Storm Lake, IA 50588

(888) SLC-IOWA or (712) 732-3780

Hours: Always visible

Cost: Free

www.stormlake.org/city/pages/treemuseum.htm

Directions: Three blocks west of Lake Ave. on Lakeshore Dr., on the north side of the lake.

TURIN
The remains of four 5,500-year-old humans were uncovered by a road crew north of Turin in 1955. Dubbed (collectively) Turin Man, they were, until recently, the oldest human remains uncovered in North America.

Washta
The Schmidt Tombstones

Many people from Washta suspected that Will Florence murdered Heinrich and Olga Schmidt with an ax. The farmhand disappeared the same day he withdrew all his savings from a local bank, which was also the same day the couple was last seen alive. Three days later the Schmidts were found dead in their kitchen, and their money was gone. Florence was later captured in Nebraska and extradited to Cherokee County, but there was never enough evidence to charge him with the killings, so he was released.

Then something odd began happening at the local cemetery. The Schmidts' white marble tombstone began to discolor, and little by little an image of Will Florence's face began to appear in the stain. Were the Schmidts trying to point an accusatory finger from the grave? Many locals were convinced and encouraged law enforcement officials to reopen the case against Florence. New evidence implicated the drifter, but by then his trail had grown cold. Nobody was ever tried for the Schmidts' murder, but their tombstone is still marked with its otherworldly clue.

Washta Cemetery, Lincoln St., Washta, IA 51061

No phone

Hours: Daily 8 A.M.–6 P.M.

Cost: Free

Directions: Head north on Lincoln St. (Rte. 31), then turn right on the first road after the bridge.

WALL LAKE

Singer **Andy Williams** was born in Wall Lake on December 3, 1927, and lived here until he was eight. His home (102 E. First Street, (712) 664-2119) is open to the public on weekends during the summer.

Wall Lake has no lake. It was drained years ago.

WASHTA

On January 12, 1912, the temperature reached £47°F in Washta, the lowest temperature ever recorded in Iowa.

Eighth Wonder of the World. Second Wonder of Iowa (after the Cheeto).

West Bend
Grotto of the Redemption

For 42 years Father Paul Dobberstein slaved away at the Grotto of the Redemption. It was intended as a monument to the Virgin Mary, who Dobberstein believed saved his life in 1897. Doberstein arrived in West Bend a year after almost dying from pneumonia, but didn't begin work on the grotto until 1912. It all started as a fishing pond and park outside the church. The goal was to get his flock to hang around after services, and because he wasn't competing with the NFL at the time, they did. Dobberstein kept a menagerie of animals adjacent to the grotto, including a black bear, a bald eagle, swans, peacocks, and coyotes. But in 1922 the bear attacked a young girl named Venetta Goodness, and that was the end of the critters. Oddly, though, newspaper accounts of the mauling brought even *more* visitors to West Bend.

Dobberstein received most of the credit for the grotto, which was the way he wanted it. However, another man, Matt Szerensce, did most of the tough, backbreaking work. He received little mention from the not-so-humble padre, except when he was referred to as "my hired hand" and "my janitor." Father Paul was not above exaggerating his own accomplishments, once claiming that he crawled through a nine-mile cave from Custer to Rapid City, South Dakota, to drag out a stone. He said that after he emerged he had to be hospitalized for weeks, just to regain his eyesight. (Did this guy ever read the Ninth Commandment?)

Before Dobberstein's grotto was completed, the Lord called the priest home. In 1954 the work then fell into the lap of Father Louis Greving, who finished the project.

Some call the Grotto of the Redemption "The Eighth Wonder of the World"—it *is* the world's largest grotto. According to estimates, the whole thing has a geologic value of $4 million. Stalactites and stalagmites from Carlsbad Caverns, emeralds, amber, sapphires, jade, carbuncle, bloodstone, fossils, amethyst, and a chuck of Antarctica from Admiral Byrd . . . no corners have been cut in this *Land of the Lost*-ish monument of religious devotion. But what did Father Dobberstein think was the most remarkable feature of the Grotto? The "imperishableness" of it.

Don't expect to understand the guy by reading the pamphlets in the geode-covered gift shop. Here are a few of Dobberstein's odd observations:

➡ "The love of precious stones is deeply implanted in the human heart."

➡ "[The grotto] will utterly confound the superstitions of those pitifully narrow-minded persons who believe in the mystic powers of precious stones."

➡ "Forgive us our effeminacy, our luxury, our lust."

➡ "Mary gave birth to Jesus in a cave in Bethlehem."

➡ "[L]et us ask those who are inclined to be critical not to be scandalized by the gorgeously rich setting which is here given the destitute little Redeemer of the World in His stable."

Whatever.

If you'd like to spend the night, there are *free* campsites on the north side of the grotto. Be aware that you'll have to put up with the floodlights and heavenly chimes until 11 P.M.

300 N. Broadway, PO Box 376, West Bend, IA 50597

(800) 868-3641 or (515) 887-2371; Gift Shop, (515) 887-5591; Restaurant, (515) 887-3591

E-mail: grotto@ncn.net

Hours: Always visible; lights out at 11 P.M.; Call for specific hours on Tours, May–October; Museum, Year-round; Gift Shop, Year-round; Restaurant, May–October; Masses, Sunday 7 A.M. and 9 A.M.

Cost: Suggested tour donation, Adults $5, Kids $2.50

www.westbendgrotto.com

Directions: Three blocks west of Rte. 15 (Tenth Ave.) on Second St. NW.

GAGA FOR GROTTOS

For those of you who appreciate Father Dobberstein's work, there are three more extant sites (there were seven at one time) where he applied his handicraft, though not on such a grand scale. Most were built in pieces in West Bend, then transported to their destinations and assembled.

★ **Dubuque:** Grotto at Mt. St. Francis Convent (3390 Windsor Avenue)

★ **Humboldt:** Memorial Fountain at John Brown Park (Fifth Street at Second Avenue)

★ **Old Rolfe:** World War II War Memorial (450th Street and 325th Avenue, northeast of Rolfe)

Regarding the construction of the grotto at Mt. St. Francis Convent, a nun's journal revealed that ". . . volunteers were . . . needed to carry the heavy slabs from the truck. . . . Sr. Catherine . . . and I were the novices selected for the job. [W]e joyfully and with much chatter began carrying the slabs. What a surprise when Father took our first slabs and said, 'Quit talking! I can't think when you talk!' That was my first lesson in observing The Great Silence."

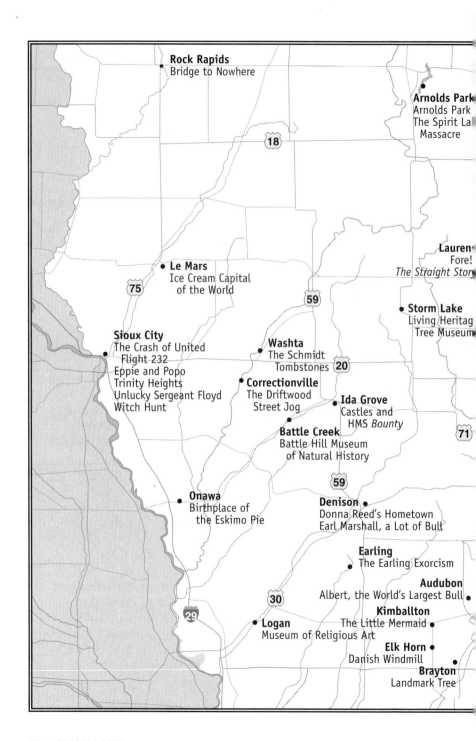

Rock Rapids
Bridge to Nowhere

Arnolds Park
Arnolds Park
The Spirit La
Massacre

18

Lauren
Fore!
The Straight Stor

Le Mars
Ice Cream Capital
of the World

75

59

Storm Lake
Living Heritag
Tree Museum

Sioux City
The Crash of United
Flight 232
Eppie and Popo
Trinity Heights
Unlucky Sergeant Floyd
Witch Hunt

Washta
The Schmidt
Tombstones

20

Correctionville
The Driftwood
Street Jog

Ida Grove
Castles and
HMS *Bounty*

Battle Creek
Battle Hill Museum
of Natural History

71

59

Onawa
Birthplace of
the Eskimo Pie

Denison
Donna Reed's Hometown
Earl Marshall, a Lot of Bull

Earling
The Earling Exorcism

30

Audubon
Albert, the World's Largest Bull

29

Kimballton
The Little Mermaid

Logan
Museum of Religious Art

Elk Horn
Danish Windmill

Brayton
Landmark Tree

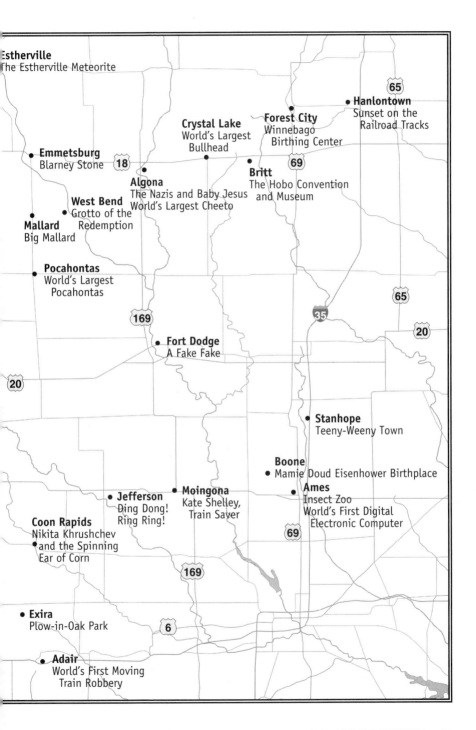

Estherville
The Estherville Meteorite

Hanlontown
Sunset on the
Railroad Tracks

65

Crystal Lake
World's Largest
Bullhead

Forest City
Winnebago
Birthing Center

Emmetsburg
Blarney Stone

18

69

Algona
The Nazis and Baby Jesus
World's Largest Cheeto

Britt
The Hobo Convention
and Museum

West Bend
Grotto of the
Redemption

Mallard
Big Mallard

Pocahontas
World's Largest
Pocahontas

65

169

35

20

20

Fort Dodge
A Fake Fake

Stanhope
Teeny-Weeny Town

Boone
Mamie Doud Eisenhower Birthplace

Jefferson
Ding Dong!
Ring Ring!

Moingona
Kate Shelley,
Train Saver

Ames
Insect Zoo
World's First Digital
Electronic Computer

Coon Rapids
Nikita Khrushchev
and the Spinning
Ear of Corn

69

169

Exira
Plow-in-Oak Park

6

Adair
World's First Moving
Train Robbery

2

THE NORTHEAST

*I*f there's a cultural Mecca in Iowa, it has to be the northeast corner of the state. Where did Antonín Dvořák flee to finish his "New World Symphony"? Where did Hollywood come to film *Field of Dreams* and *Twister*? Where did kooky Wisconsin art student Luke Helder decide to place the left eye of his smiley face portrait during his nationwide mailbox-bombing campaign of May 3–6, 2002? The answer to these questions is the same: northeast Iowa.

Yes, other parts of the state might brag about being the birthplace of Johnny Carson or Tom Arnold or Dear Abby, but northeast Iowa has the World's Largest Matchstick Replica of the U.S. Capitol Building, the marionettes from *The Sound of Music*, a burned and water-damaged replica of half of the Gutenberg Bible, and the state's most elaborate treehouse. Top them cultural apples!

Well, I just might. See for yourself. . . .

Anamosa
Anamosa State Penitentiary Museum

Sad as it is, incarceration has become one of this nation's booming industries. Want to see how it's done, or at least how it's been done over the years? Stop on by the Anamosa State Penitentiary Museum. Housed in the prison's old cheese factory, the museum has a replica cell (only four by nine feet in size), a diorama showing convicts pounding rocks in a quarry, and an impressive collection of prisoners crafts—known as "shanks" in prison lingo. There's also a gift shop if you're interested.

Though this prison, sometimes referred to as the White Palace of the West (mostly by folks *outside* its walls), was built in 1872, it's still open for business with around 1,200 inmates. The structure was built using prison labor, and they did such a nice job that it became a tourist destination: around the turn of the century, visitors could pay 25¢ to walk through. And in 1935 the movie *Penitentiary* was filmed here, the first feature-length film ever shot in Iowa. Nothing like showing your best face to the world!

406 N. High St., Anamosa, IA 52205

(319) 462-2386

E-mail: aspmuseum@aol.com

Hours: June–September, Friday–Sunday Noon–4 P.M.

Cost: Adults $2.50, Kids Free

www.asphistory.com/museum

Directions: Three blocks west of Rte. X31 and three blocks north of Rte. E28 (Main St.), on the north side of the prison.

NOT EXACTLY A SUCCESS STORY

The Anamosa State Penitentiary doesn't exactly have a spotless record when it comes to rehabilitating its inmates. In 1968 **John Wayne Gacy**, manager of a Kentucky Fried Chicken in Waterloo, was convicted of sexually assaulting a minor. He served an 18-month sentence and, upon his release, moved to Illinois. And he got into a *lot* of trouble.

Born to be filed.
Photo by author, courtesy of National Motorcycle Museum and Hall of Fame.

Captain America's Deathbike

For years *Easy Rider's* Captain America (played by Peter Fonda) has come to epitomize the wandering spirit lured by the adventure of the open road. (Of course, when Captain America is murdered by a bunch of rednecks at the end of the flick, the thought of hitting the highway suddenly seems less romantic.) The chopper used for the movie's final crash sequence was given to actor Dan "Grizzly Adams" Haggerty, who restored it to its original condition. It is now the star attraction at the National Motorcycle Museum & Hall of Fame in Anamosa.

Captain America's deathbike is only a small part of this amazing collection. They've also got Steve McQueen's 1947 Indian Chief, along with his dirty bedroll, and Evel Knievel's 1972 Harley-Davidson XR750. There are more than 170 bikes on display, some of them on loan from collectors, as well as hundreds of trophies, toys, helmets, engines, and paintings that trace the history of the motorcycle back more than a century. This museum was originally located in Sturgis, South Dakota—ground zero for motorcycle aficionados—but today it's here in the heart of the Midwest.

National Motorcycle Museum & Hall of Fame, 200 E. Main St., PO Box 405, Anamosa, IA 52205

(319) 462-3925

E-mail: national_mc_museum@hotmail.com

Hours: April–October, Monday–Saturday 9 A.M.–5 P.M., Sunday 10 A.M.–4 P.M.; November–March , Monday–Friday 9 A.M.–5 P.M., Saturday 10 A.M.–4 P.M., Sunday 11 A.M.–4 P.M.

Cost: Adults $5, Seniors (60+) $4, Kids (12 and under) Free (with adult)

www.nationalmuseum.org

Directions: One blocks east of Rte. X31 on Rte. E28 (Main St.).

AMANA COLONIES
The Amana Colonies claim to be the Bratwurst Capital of the World.

When the Amana Colonies were founded in 1855, all musical instruments were banned, except the flute.

Members of Amana's Community of True Inspiration were not buried side-by-side with family members, but in chronological order according to their deaths.

BELLE PLAINE
In 1886 a crew digging a well at Eighth Avenue and Eighth Street in Belle Plaine struck an artesian aquifer. The gusher, dubbed the Jumbo Well, spurted 5–9 million gallons of water *each day* until it was capped a year later.

Sign, sign, everywhere a sign.

Belle Plaine
George's Filling Station

Until the day he died in 1993, George Preston maintained that his Belle Plaine gas station was the last original fill-'er-up on the Old Lincoln Highway. Lincoln Highway opened in 1913 and became known as the Main Street of America; it was the nation's first intercontinental highway. It still stretches from New York's Times Square to San Francisco's Lincoln Park, and, for you map-reading nuts, Belle Plaine marks the midway point between Chicago and Omaha.

Preston opened George's Filling Station in 1923 and ran it for the next seven decades. Over the years he mounted hundreds of advertising signs on the station's outer walls, and the interior, too. You'll only get to see the signs on the exterior, however, because George's Filling Station is now closed for business. It makes a nice photo stop, though.

Twelfth St. and Fourth Ave., Belle Plaine, IA 52208

(319) 434-6458

Hours: Always visible

Cost: Free

www.lincolnhighwayassoc.org/iowa

Directions: Three blocks west of Rte. 21 (Seventh Ave.) on Rte. 131 (Twelfth St.).

Brooklyn
The Community of Flags

These days it seems *every* community is bedecked with banners, but Brooklyn was the Community of Flags long before it became a national fixation. And, unlike other towns, Brooklyn has banners of other nations, and not just from the Coalition of the Willing. They've got every American state flag surrounding Old Glory in a park on the main drag, and 35 selected country flags along Jackson Street. It probably goes without saying, but unless the wind is blowing, Brooklyn is barely worth the stop.

Third and Jackson Sts., Brooklyn, IA 52211

(641) 522-5300

E-mail: brkchmbr@netins.net

Hours: Always visible

Cost: Free

www.brooklyniowa.com

Directions: Most flags are along Rtes. V18 and F29.

Burr Oak
The Little Hotel in the Village

Readers of Laura Ingalls Wilder's books probably feel they have an accurate chronology of her young life. However, there were two years that went missing from her book series, between *On the Banks of Plum Creek* and *By the Shores of Silver Lake*. They were the two years her family spent in Burr Oak, Iowa.

The Ingalls family fled Walnut Grove, Minnesota, during the 1876 locust plague, heading east. Pa had been hired to manage the eleven-room Masters Hotel in Burr Oak by its new owner, William Steadman, a friend from Walnut Grove and fellow grasshopper refugee. This was long before child-labor laws, and nine-year-old Laura was put into service cooking, cleaning, and waiting tables when she wasn't attending school.

Ma and Pa weren't happy about the fact that a saloon was attached to the hotel, though Laura was secretly fascinated by a hole in the kitchen door where a drunken patron had once taken a shot at his fleeing wife. Eventually the family moved next door to a room above the Kimball Grocery (since torn down), and none too soon. In the winter of 1877 the saloon caught fire, though it did not spread to the hotel. Later that spring a skinny barhound whom everyone called Hairpin died under mysterious circumstances; it was likely alcohol poisoning from a three-day bender, but some claimed his lungs were immolated when he tried to light a cigar and the alcohol on his breath ignited. The Ingallses resolved to move even farther away, and rented a brick house on Waters Street on the northwest side of town (also torn down).

When the locust plague ended in 1878, the family returned to Walnut Grove. Since Laura never mentioned Burr Oak in her books, the site was almost lost to posterity. But during the 1970s, researchers located the hotel, purchased it with the help of schoolchildren, and restored it to its 1870s appearance. The Masters Hotel is the only home from Laura's childhood that is still standing. Burr Oak hosts Laura Ingalls Wilder Days each June, with a popular Little Miss Laura contest.

Laura Ingalls Wilder Park and Museum, 3603 236th Ave., Burr Oak, IA 52101

Contact: PO Box 354, Decorah, IA 52101

(563) 735-5916

E-mail: museum@lauraingallswilder.us

Hours: May–October, Monday–Saturday 9 A.M.–5 P.M., Sunday Noon–4 P.M.;
   November–April, Thursday–Saturday 10 A.M.–3 P.M.

Cost: Adults $5, Seniors (60+) $4, Kids (6–17) $3, Families $12

www.lauraingallswilder.us

Directions: One block east of Rte. 52.

Cedar Falls
Ice Is Nice!

Anyone who's ever toured a local history museum has no doubt had this experience: a retired tour guide leads you over to an icebox and says, "We didn't have refrigerators in those days—we had *iceboxes*, and you had to buy ice to keep your food cold. I bet you never knew *that*!" Well, you probably did, but you grinned and prayed that there wasn't also a clothes wringer, a butter churn, or a wood-burning stove on the tour.

So, Mr. or Ms. Know-It-All, there's nothing you don't know about ice, right? Step into the Ice House Museum and you might be surprised. Built in 1921, this round building once supplied ice to Cedar Falls and its surrounding communities. Blocks were harvested from the Cedar River during the winter using horse-drawn ice plows (did you know that, hmmmm?), then carted here on sleds. The blocks were stacked all the way up to the rafters, separated by layers of insulating straw. This enormous, 100-foot-diameter structure could hold between 6,000 and 8,000 *tons* of ice when fully packed. The Cedar Falls Ice House didn't have much of a working life; due to the advent of modern appliances, it closed for good in 1934.

This museum isn't just a tribute to water in its solid form. A Hollywoodish Cedar Falls backdrop lines the circular walls of this structure, giving you a chance to see turn-of-the-century versions of a barber shop, a doctor's office, and a broom making shop. Did you know that brooms were once woven by hand?

Hey . . . where are you going?

Ice House Museum, W. First and Franklin Sts., Cedar Falls, IA 50613

Contact: Cedar Falls Historical Society, 303 Franklin St., Cedar Falls, IA 50613

(319) 266-5149

E-mail: cfhs_schmitz@cfu.net

Hours: May–October, Wednesday, Saturday–Sunday 2–4:30 P.M.

Cost: Free

www.cedarfallshistorical.org/ice_house_museum.htm

Directions: Where Rte. 218 (Center St.) meets Rte. 57 (First St.), at the river.

CEDAR RAPIDS

Actor **Ron Livingston** was born in Cedar Rapids on June 5, 1968, but grew up in Marion.

Fifteen trees in a Cedar Rapids city park were recently found fitted with doorknobs and locks. Each tree had two knobs, one in front and one in back. The mysterious locksmith was never found. Police said it was either a prank or "an ambitious squirrel."

Some Cedar Rapids residents call themselves Bunnies, a pun based on the city's pronunciation, as in See-der Rabbits.

Something for Mary.

Cedar Rapids
Our Lady of Sorrows Grotto

William Lightner converted to Catholicism at the age of 33, and, boy, did he convert. In 1929 he was building Warde Hall on the campus of Mt. Mercy College and he asked the nuns if there was something more he could do to demonstrate his faith. "A grotto to the Virgin Mary would be nice," someone suggested, and away Lightner flew like lightning. A grotto—that's it!

And what a grotto it turned out to be. For the next dozen years he spent all his free time, energy, and money to turn 1,200 *tons* of rocks and semiprecious stones into a massive garden grotto. The centerpiece was a 10-pillar monument, each column representing a different commandment. It was surrounded by a geode-encrusted bridge, two elaborate arches, stone fences, and a reflecting pool.

The grotto was dedicated in 1941, but Lightner wasn't finished. Not until the Sisters of Mercy threatened him with merciless legal action did this dedicated man put down his trowel for good. Had he been allowed to work on it until his death in 1968, there might not have been as much need for restoration in 2002. The main grotto wall and the reflecting pool are long gone, but the Ten Commandments and the Bridge of Life are still around, and you're welcome to visit.

Mt. Mercy College, 1330 Elmhurst Dr. NE, Cedar Rapids, IA 52402

(800) 248-4504 or (319) 363-1323

Hours: Always visible

Cost: Free

www2.mtmercy.edu/campusmap.html (click on Grotto)

Directions: On the southwest side of campus, two blocks east of Oakland Rd. NE, three blocks south of 29th St. NE, just south of Warde Hall.

Tahitian Room and Grizzly Bar

Pop culture historians trace America's affection for tiki lounges to nostalgic World War II vets who served in the South Pacific. Though they flourished in the 1950s, there were almost no tiki bars before the mid-1940s, *except* in one Cedar Falls mansion.

Brucemore was built in the 1800s by the Sinclair family. Its Queen Anne–style exterior camouflages the renovations made in 1937 by its third owner, Howard Hall. This lounge lizard luminary installed a Tahitian Room with island dioramas in the portholes, sculpted hula girls, and a map of Tahiti and Moorea painted on the floor. When you flipped a switch you'd hear the pinging of raindrops on the tin roof over your head. Miracle of nature? No, just an indoor sprinkler system that recycled the "rain" after it ran off the roof of the Tahitian Room's hut.

Hall didn't just have a Polynesian flair. He also built a Grizzly Bar with a North Woods motif. Spittoons are scattered here and there, the walls are lined with aspen logs, and a pile of poker chips sits atop a table waiting for a little Yukon recreation.

The Hall family's eccentricities extended to their menagerie of pets, which included an African lion named Leo, son of the famous MGM lion, Jackie. Leo is buried in Brucemore's garden, along with numerous dogs and a second lion who succeeded Leo. You're welcome to pay your respects during the tour.

Brucemore, 2160 Linden Dr. SE, Cedar Rapids, IA 52403

(319) 362-7375

E-mail: mail@brucemore.org

Hours: February–December, Tuesday–Saturday, 10 A.M.–3 P.M., Sunday Noon–3 P.M.;
tours on the hour

Cost: Adults $7, Kids (6–18) $3

www.brucemore.org

Directions: One block southeast of First Ave. NE (Rte.151) on 20th St. NE.

Decorah
Rocks and Bugs

If the Iowa State Rock is the geode—and it is—then the fence surrounding Decorah's Porter House Museum must be the Iowa State Fence: it's covered with the crystal-filled stones. This odd structure was built over the course of six years by Adelbert Field Porter, a local naturalist.

Porter wasn't just a geologic nerd; he was also interested in winged insects and postage stamps. His impressive collection of mounted bugs is still on display, long after his death, as well as his rocks, minerals, and first day covers (if you're not a philatelist, don't ask). Be sure to look for Porter's Flintstonesque rock lamp during your visit.

Porter House Museum, 401 W. Broadway, Decorah, IA 52101

(563) 382-8465

Hours: May–December, Tuesday–Saturday 9 A.M.–4 P.M., Sunday Noon–4 P.M.

Cost: Adults $5, Seniors $4, Kids (6–16) $3

Directions: Two blocks south of Water St. (Rte. W20), one block east of Mechanic St.

CLINTON
A seven-foot-tall Bigfoot has been spotted in the Bulgar's Hollow Recreation Area, just north of Clinton.

It isn't the length but the elevation that matters.

Dubuque
The Fenelon Place Elevator

Sometimes a nap can be very productive. Case in point? The Fenelon Place Elevator. Back in 1882, banker J. K. Graves had a problem: he worked in downtown Dubuque but his home was two and a half blocks away . . . at the top of the bluff. If he wanted to go home for a lunchtime nap, the long buggy trip home and back ate up an hour of his 90-minute siesta. Graves had seen a cog railway on a trip to Europe and figured, "Heck, why not build one of my own?" The cable-powered contraption was designed and built by John Bell and was soon lifting Graves 189 feet in elevation along 296 feet of track to his home and bed. Nobody realized it at the time, but Graves's contraption turned out to be the shortest and steepest inclined railway in the world! (It still holds that record.)

Though it originated as a private conveyance, the neighbors kept bumming rides off Graves. After an 1884 fire, the rebuilt elevator was opened to the public at 5¢ a ride. The railway burned again in 1893, but by then the locals had grown to depend upon it. Graves was broke, so the Fenelon Place Elevator Company, with ten stockholders, was formed to rebuild the device. The new railway had two counterbalanced cars: when one was at the top, the other was at the bottom. This two-car arrangement is the same today. The operator's house burned in 1962 (what's with this place?), and the whole structure was refurbished in 1977.

If you start your ride at the bottom, just hop into a car and ring the bell. An operator at the top of the bluff will then engage the motor and you'll be at the summit a minute later, just in time for your own nap.

512 Fenelon Place, Dubuque, IA 52001

(563) 582-6496

E-mail: fenelonplaceelev@qwest.net

Hours: April–November, daily 8 A.M.–10 P.M.

Cost: Round trip, Adults $1.50, Kids (5–12) 50¢; One way, Adults 75¢, Kids 25¢

www.dbq.com/fenplco

Directions: At Fourth St. and Bluff St., one block west of Locust St.

DUBUQUE

A Dubuque foreman at the Novelty Iron Works found several live frogs frozen in hailstones that fell on June 16, 1882.

Mathias Ham House

In 1856 Mathias Ham built a beautiful home in Dubuque that overlooked the Mississippi River. It was widely admired as the most elegant home in town. From his vantage point near the bluff, Ham not only could survey the entire river, but he could also spot, and report, pirate activity. Several of the marauders were sent to jail, but not before vowing to return one day and exact their revenge on the guy who turned them in.

It took them a while. Nearly fifty years later, after Ham and his first and second wives had died, and after all but one of his children, Sarah, had croaked or moved away, the pirates returned. Sarah Ham heard footsteps in the house downstairs, and when they came to a stop outside her bedroom door, she fired her gun. The wounded intruder fled but was found dead near the river's edge.

According to legend, the pirate's spirit still haunts Ham House. He's a talented ghost: he plays the house's organ—and the organ is busted! He also opens doors and flicks on lights that have no fuses. And he is said to guard a treasure hidden at the far end of a collapsed tunnel leading away from the cellar. Ask your costumed guide all about it.

2241 Lincoln Ave. Dubuque, IA 52001

(800) 226-3369 or (319) 583-2812

Hours: May–October, daily 10 A.M.–4:30 P.M.

Cost: Adults $3.50, Kids $1.50, Family $10

www.mississippirivermuseum.com/hamhouse.htm

Directions: Head north on Rte. 3 to Rhomberg Ave., then east to Shiras Ave., then north one block to Lincoln Ave.

Dyersville
Field of Dreams, Fields of Nightmares

If you build it, they will come. But if you plow it under, they will be *really* ticked off. That's the lesson learned by the Lansing family, owners of half of Dyersville's Field of Dreams.

The 1989 movie's baseball field was actually cobbled together using land from two different Dyersville farms. Don and Becky Lansing owned the farmhouse, the diamond, and right field, while Al and Rita Ameskamp owned the rest. Shortly after filming wrapped, the Ameskamps replanted center and left fields in corn, and the Lansings did the same with right field. (The year the movie was filmed was Iowa's worst drought since the Dust Bowl, and both families were fortunate that producers pumped in enough water to make the remaining crop look presentable. Their neighbors weren't so lucky.)

When movie lovers started showing up by the carload, the Lansings rebuilt their half of the ballpark, but the Ameskamps didn't budge; they wanted part of the action from the gift shop. Fans of mythical baseball were disappointed to see only half the dreamy field, and eventually the Ameskamps relented . . . and opened their own gift shop. The Lansings incorporated as the Field of Dreams Movie Site while the Ameskamps became the Left and Center Field of Dreams. In 1999 the Ameskamps requested and received a rezoning permit to plow a Shoeless Joe Jackson–shaped maze behind left field for folks to traipse through, which ticked off the Lansings even more.

You're not likely to pick up on all the bad blood simmering just beneath the surface here, nor should you bring up the issue—just enjoy the ballpark. If you come the last Sunday of any summer month, you can see the cast's original Ghost Players emerge from the corn and play a pick-up game from noon to 2 P.M., referred to as the "Greatest Show on Dirt."

Field of Dreams Movie Site, 28963 Lansing Rd., Dyersville, IA 52040
(888) 875-8404 or (563) 875-8404
E-mail: shoelessjoe@fieldofdreammoviesite.com
Hours: April–November, daily 9 A.M.–6 P.M.
Cost: Free
www.fieldofdreamsmoviesite.com
Directions: Head north from town on Rte. 136 (Fifth Ave. NE), which turns into Dyersville East Rd.; drive for three miles, then turn right on Lansing Rd.

Left and Center Field of Dreams, 29001 Lansing Rd., Dyersville, IA 52040
(800) 443-8981 or (563) 875-7985
E-mail: dreams@mwci.net
Hours: June–August, daily 9 A.M.–8 P.M.; April–May and September–November, daily 9 A.M.–6 P.M.
Cost: Free; Maze, Adults $6, Kids (12 and under) $4
www.leftandcenterfod.com
Directions: Head north from town on Rte. 136 (Fifth Ave. NE), which turns into Dyersville East Rd.; drive for three miles, then turn right on Lansing Rd.

National Farm Toy Museum

The bottom may have fallen out of the Beanie Baby market, but farm toys are still going strong, at least in this part of the country. The Ertl Company has been manufacturing die-cast tractors, combines, and more for half a century, and every model they ever made is here on display. But that's not all—this museum has more than 30,000 toy samples from other companies as well! There's even a 1950s Ertl assembly line where you can imagine yourself spending eight hours a day fitting widgets together.

The museum's collection isn't strictly agricultural; it also has toy golf carts, fire engines, Dairy Queen blimps, banks, and small-scale hearses. The museum's second floor contains a series of dioramas made by Everett and Myra Weber on the history of corn and grain harvesting. Their survey starts with the Egyptians and the Chinese and continues through today's corporate farms. Fans of children's pedal tractors will also find an impressive display here.

1110 16th Ave. Court SE, Dyersville, IA 52040

(563) 875-2727

E-mail: farmtoys@dyersville.net

Hours: Daily 8 A.M.–7 P.M.

Cost: Adults $4, Kids (6–11) $1

www.nftonline.com

Directions: Head north on Rte. 136 from Rte. 20, turn right on 15th Ave., then right on 11th St. SE to 16th Ave. Ct.

DUBUQUE

Actress **Kate Mulgrew** was born in Dubuque on April 29, 1955.

Actor **Don Ameche**, who died on December 6, 1993, is buried in Dubuque's Resurrection Catholic Cemetery (4300 Asbury Road).

Iowa's first legal execution, that of convicted murderer Patrick O'Connor, took place in 1834 at the corner of White and Seventh streets in Dubuque.

Not blown away . . . yet.

Eldora
Twister House

Visit Iowa in the summer and it's entirely possible that you'll come across a home damaged by a tornado. But if you travel to Eldora, you're *sure* to see one. However, the 1891 house on Y Avenue southeast of town wasn't trashed by a real tornado, but by a fake one created by a special effects crew for the movie *Twister*. The old home and barn were restored from their rundown appearance, then trashed again for filming. The imploded barn was never rebuilt, but the pile of rubble has been left intact by owner Chuck Welch.

The *Twister* house was repainted after filming, and the broken windows were replaced. The rest of the farm remains pretty much the way it looked when the crew jetted back to Hollywood. They even left the pyrotechnic control panel for the exploding fence.

Welch has reopened the home as a bed and breakfast, but it's rather rustic. Take the tour and he'll show you a scrapbook of the 1997 and 2000 twisters that blew through the area. Remember, the movie was released in 1996—these other two storms were *real*. Enjoy your stay!

26302 Y Ave., Eldora, IA 50627

(641) 858-5133

Hours: Call ahead for tours or B&B reservations

Cost: Tours, $2; Rooms, $25–$50/night

http://eldora.net/twister

Directions: East from Eldora three miles on Rte. 175, then south two miles on Y Ave.

Have a seat, Leif.

Elma
Viking Throne Chairs

For years Norwegian Americans have been trying to convince us that the Vikings discovered America long before Columbus. As proof, they often point to any number of "artifacts," most of which have been found, coincidentally, by Norwegian Americans.

Two such artifacts are the Viking "throne chairs" in Elma Park. If the stories are to be believed, these stone chairs were carved by explorers years ago so that they would have a place to sit. A researcher of antiquities has claimed that these concave seats were once covered in a plaster-like substance made from blood, resin, milk, aluminum, and silica. Obviously, this was in an era before Scotchguard.

Sounds pretty far-fetched to me. Imagine, just for a moment, that you are thousands of miles from your homeland, having rowed across the Atlantic and marched into the middle of a continent inhabited by a native population with whom you are unable to communicate—would you expend the time and energy it must have taken to chip these ancient La-Z-Boys out of a pair of boulders? Wouldn't a log have worked just as well? I'm only asking.

Elma Park, Rtes. B17 and V18, Elma, IA 50628

No phone

Hours: Always visible

Cost: Free

Directions: On the southwest corner of Rte. V18 (Busti Ave.) and Rte. B17.

Festina
World's Smallest Church

When 16-year-old Johann Gaertner was drafted into Napoleon's army, his mother was distraught. She pleaded with God, "If Johann returns safely, I will build a shrine to the Virgin Mary." And though Johann survived, his mother did not. Johann emigrated to the United States in 1840, and moved to Iowa in 1851. Throughout his life he repeated the story of his deliverance, downplaying the promise his mother was never able to keep.

In 1885, while visiting an old mission cemetery west of Festina, his daughter, Mary Ann Huber, snapped. "Put up or shut up!" she demanded (or something like that). Johann was 92 years old at the time, so Mary Ann volunteered her husband, Frank Joseph Huber, to help. With several more workers, the pair quarried stone from nearby Snake Hollow and constructed the St. Anthony of Padua Chapel. It wasn't big—only 14 by 20 feet—but it got Johann off the hook with the Big Guy upstairs. Both Gaertner and Frank Huber died two years later.

The World's Smallest Church sits on the site of two previous chapels. The first, built by a Father Petiot in 1842, was burned to the ground by a rival missionary, Reverend Lowry. (The Presbyterian minister thought the priest was cutting into his business converting the Winnebago Indians.)

A log church, Our Lady of Seven Dolors, was then erected here in 1849. Its large wooden cross was struck by lightning in the 1850s, and the chapel was eventually abandoned. Whether the lightning bolt had anything to do with the congregation's departure is unclear. However, the splintered cross was kept by the followers and placed beneath the floor of St. Anthony of Padua, where it remains to this day.

Descendants of Gaertner and Huber still maintain the World's Smallest Church. If you're planning a visit, please note that the place only seats eight.

St. Anthony of Padua Chapel, Little Church Rd., Festina, IA 52144

(319) 382-3990

Hours: Daylight

Cost: Free

Directions: East of Festina one mile on 123rd St., then south one mile on Little Church Rd.

Froelich
Birthplace of the Tractor

In the late 1800s John Froelich owned a successful grain elevator in a small town named after his father, and he rented out a steam-powered combine to farmers on the side. Steam combines were notoriously dangerous—their boilers often exploded—and they were also known to ignite prairie fires when cinders blew up their smokestacks and landed on dry wheat fields in autumn. This tended to anger farmers.

So in 1892 Froelich, with the help of employee Will Mann, came up with a contraption with a newfangled gasoline engine that could drive both forward *and* backward and could be hooked up to power a combine. It worked well enough, and a year later he formed the Waterloo Gasoline Traction Engine Company. Froelich and Mann built only four gasoline traction engines before the company was sold off to a group of investors who renamed the operation the Waterloo Gasoline Engine Company. (How original!) Froelich eventually moved to St. Paul, Minnesota, where he worked as a financial advisor.

There was one piece of advice Froelich might have offered to his clients: *don't sell your interest in a potential goldmine!* His former business struggled along for a few years under its new ownership until the group came up with the Waterloo Boy Model R. They sold over 4,500

Waterloo Boys in 1917. This caught the attention of John Deere, and in 1918 Deere purchased the company for $2.35 million (a lot of money back then).

Today there's a historic monument on the site of Froelich's old elevator, and a small tractor museum next door. Any of Froelich's descendants who stop by for a visit are permitted to weep openly when they realize the inheritance that could have been theirs.

Froelich Foundation General Store and Tractor History Museum, 24397 Froelich Rd., Froelich, IA 51257

(563) 536-2841

E-mail: rjswarr1@netins.net

Hours: June–October, Thursday–Tuesday 11 A.M.–5 P.M.

Cost: Free

Directions: Nine miles west of McGregor on Rte. 18, just west of Rte. 52.

MORE TRACTOR STUFF

★ **Atlantic:** Each year Atlantic High School (1201 E. 14th Street, (712) 243-5358) hosts Tractor Day, when students are encouraged to drive their families' tractors to class.

★ **Charles City:** Charles Hart and Charles Parr started the Hart-Parr Gasoline Engine Traction Company in Charles City in 1900. Sales "manager W. H. Williams came up with the term "tractor" in 1907, which is shorthand for "gasoline traction engine." You can see a 1913 Hart-Parr, the twelfth ever built, at the Floyd County Historical Society Museum (500 Gilbert Street, (641) 228-1099, www.floydcounty museum.org).

★ **Mitchell:** The 4140 Reeves tractor at the Cedar Valley Memories Museum in Mitchell (18791 Route 9, (641) 732-1269) was built in 1912 and is the World's Largest Steam-Powered Tractor. It stands two stories tall and requires a pair of people to operate.

★ **Nemaha:** A group of eight men from Nemaha perform the Farmall Tractor Promenade each year, the world's only tractor square dance. Four men wear dresses and drive six-horsepower "C" Farmalls; the other four drive twenty-five-horsepower "H" Farmalls.

Gladbrook
Matchstick Marvels

Three cheers for Patrick Acton and the visionary folks of Gladbrook!
While so many other odd and unique museums have faded into obscurity, this community has actually rallied around Acton's wonderfully weird obsession: creating scale models of famous buildings out of matchsticks. Big deal, you say? Wait until you see them. . . .

Acton's largest creation is a replica of the U.S. Capitol; it's 12 feet long, 5 feet tall, and took about 478,000 matchsticks to complete. Get the idea? His Space Shuttle *Challenger* (complete with launching pad) took only about 200,000 matchsticks. For each model Acton has tabulated the number of matchsticks and hours that have gone into building it. The USS *Iowa* battleship: 137,000 matchsticks/800 hours. The brontosaurus: 10,000 matchsticks/150 hours. Iowa's governor's residence, Terrace Hill: 193,000 matchsticks/800 hours. And the Notre Dame cathedral: 174,000 matchsticks/2,000 hours. Acton used a single red matchstick on the cathedral, which he invites visitors to search for.

Though some of Acton's larger works are housed in Ripley's Believe It Or Not! museums around the nation, the bulk of his 30 years of toil are located in this brand-new, well-designed museum in the Gladbrook Community Theater and Tourist Center. Fans of the bizarre should put this place on their Iowa itinerary.

319 Second St., Gladbrook, IA 50635

(888) 473-3456 or (641) 473-2410

E-mail: matchstickmarvels@hotmail.com

Hours: April–November, daily 1–5 P.M.

Cost: Adults $2, Kids (5–12) $1

www.matchstickmarvels.com

Directions: Downtown between Spring and Gould Sts.

Guttenberg
Gutenberg Bible

Between 1450 and 1456 Johann Gutenberg printed 100 or so Bibles in Mainz, Germany. By modern standards his output was pitiful, but considering he was also inventing the first printing press with movable type at the time, it's probably OK to cut him some slack. More than five centuries later, only 46 of those original Gutenberg Bibles are known to exist. The Bible in the Guttenberg Public Library is not one of them.

Though it looks very much like the original, this holy book is one of 310 two-volume tomes produced in 1913 by Insel-Verlag of Leipzig, Germany. This particular facsimile (#122) was damaged during an Allied bombing raid on August 12, 1942; you can still see the burns on the cover and the water-damaged pages.

The citizens of Guttenberg, who named their town for the man who invented modern printing, misspelled his name when they incorporated. Perhaps to make up for it, they purchased this damaged replica of his signature work in the late 1940s.

Guttenberg Public Library, 603 S. Second St., Guttenberg, IA 52052

(563) 252-3108

Hours: Monday and Wednesday 1–7:30 P.M., Tuesday and Thursday 10 A.M.–5 P.M., Saturday 9 A.M.–3 P.M.

Cost: Free

www.guttenberg-iowa.org/gutbible.htm

Directions: Three blocks east of Rte. 52 (Fifth St.), two blocks south of Herder St.

GARRISON
A flying saucer landed on the Barr family farm near Garrison on July 13, 1969. When it took off, it left a charred ring of grass.

GREEN MOUNTAIN
A train derailment in Green Mountain on March 21, 1910, killed 55 passengers.

GRINNELL
Editor **Horace Greeley** told Josiah Grinnell, "Go west, young man."

Jimmy Carter's worst nightmare.

Marquette
Pinky the Elephant

If you stumble out of the Isle of Capri Casino and come face-to-face with a large pink elephant, do not be alarmed—you're not necessarily seeing things. In all likelihood you've just met Pinky the Elephant.

Pinky has lived in Marquette for more than forty years; he was created in 1963 by local businessman Bob Reis. When President Jimmy Carter visited Prairie du Chien in August 1978, Reis taunted the Democrat by pulling Pinky up and down the Mississippi on a pair of waterskis. If Carter was angered, he never let it show, but that's the kind of guy he is. And besides, asking the Secret Service to torpedo a defenseless fiberglass creature could endanger one's chances at a Nobel Peace Prize.

For several years Pinky welcomed diners to the Pink Elephant Supper Club, but has since been appropriated by the Isle of Capri Casino. If you stumble out of the casino and see *two* Pinkys, you might want to call the Iowa Gambling Treatment Program (www.1800betsoff.org, (800) 552-4700).

Isle of Capri Casino and Hotel, 101 Antimonopoly, Marquette, IA 52158
(800) 4-YOU-BET or (563) 873-3531

E-mail: jeff_dull@islecorp.com

Hours: Always visible

Cost: Free

www.isleofcapricasino.com

Directions: Just south of Rte. 18 on Rte. 76 (First St.), at the railroad tracks.

Marshalltown
Big Treehouse

Some kids grow out of the treehouse-building stage, but not Mick Jurgensen. His family purchased the Shady Oaks Campground when he was only three years old, and he's been playing out in the shady oaks ever since. The observation "The only difference between men and boys is the price of their toys" certainly holds true in this case. In 1980 Jurgensen, by then an adult, started building a simple treehouse in his favorite grove. One platform led to another, and another, and today 5,000 square feet spread out over 12 different levels, the top 55 feet higher than the bottom. Jurgensen has installed over a dozen porch swings, a telephone, running water, a microwave, flower boxes, a grill, a sound system, and a Shady Oaks Museum in the treehouse. And in 2003 he added a handy spiral staircase for a direct route to the highest peak where visitors are invited to survey the countryside. The Swiss Family Robinson never had it so good.

The Shady Oaks Campground has been around since 1925 and was the first cabin camp along the Lincoln Highway west of the Mississippi River. Now it's the coolest.

Shady Oaks RV Park, 2370-A Shady Oaks Rd., Marshalltown, IA 50158

(641) 752-2946

E-mail: marygift@mchsi.com

Hours: May–October by appointment only

Cost: Adults $2

www.bigtreehouse.net

Directions: Three miles east of town on Rte. 30 Business (Shady Oaks Rd./240th St.).

MARSHALLTOWN
Horses may not legally eat fire hydrants in Marshalltown.

Mason City
"The Lonely Goatherd" Marionettes

Anyone watching *The Sound of Music* could be excused for thinking the marionettes in "The Lonely Goatherd" puppet show were controlled by those multitalented von Trapp children, but that would be incorrect. The strings in that show were pulled by Mason City's own Bil Baird and his wife, Cora. Never heard of them? Then stop on by the Charles H. Mac-Nider Museum.

Baird grew up in Mason City, where he was given his first puppet at the age of nine. Young Bil (who was Bill at the time) would give free puppet shows in the family's attic to anyone who would show up. His first full-length performance was *Treasure Island*. After college and five years as an apprentice to master puppeteer Tony Sarg, Baird got his first solo gig playing the 1934 Chicago World's Fair. Three years later he met his future wife and collaborator, Cora Burlar. Together they produced plays, television specials, commercials, corporate gigs, and educational government films.

The bulk of the Bairds' puppet collection, more than 400 marionettes, was donated to the museum after their deaths. Not only does the museum have the entire Goatherd ensemble on display, but there are also other favorites such as Whistling Wizard and Flannel Mouse, Snarky Parker and Birdie, Bubbles La Rue (a bare-breasted stripper), Charlemane the Lion, and the full cast of the "Winnie the Pooh and Friends" TV special.

If you're interested in fine art, the MacNider's got that, too.

Charles H. MacNider Museum, 303 Second St. SE, Mason City, IA 50401

(641) 421-3666

E-mail: macnider@macniderart.org

Hours: Tuesday and Thursday 9 A.M.–9 P.M., Wednesday, Friday–Saturday 9 A.M.–5 P.M., Sunday 1–5 P.M.

Cost: Free

www.macniderart.org

Directions: Two blocks east of Delaware Ave. (Rte. 65) on Second St. SE, at Georgia Ave.

MASON CITY
Mason City was originally named Shibboleth.

The Music Man

Mason City's Meredith Willson led a remarkable life. Just out of high school, he was selected for the John Philip Sousa Band, where he played piccolo for three years, and later joined the NBC Symphony under Arturo Toscanini. While living in New York, he was hired to play scales on his flute for Dr. Lee deForest as he developed the talking motion picture. At 33, heading west, Willson became the youngest conductor of the San Francisco Symphony Orchestra. He wrote the score for Charlie Chaplin's *The Great Dictator* and worked with George Burns and Gracie Allen, Tallulah Bankhead, Ethel Merman, and more, on the radio. He even wrote "It's Beginning to Look [a Lot] Like Christmas," the only memorable tune from a failed stage adaptation of *The Miracle on 34th Street*. But for all Willson accomplished, he's most often remembered for a single work: *The Music Man*. And well he should be; it's one of the greatest musicals ever written.

Willson started off big. Born in Mason City on May 18, 1902, he weighed 14 pounds, 6 ounces, the largest baby ever born in Iowa. The youngest of three Willson children (who grew to adulthood), Meredith was prodded into music by his demanding mother, Rosalie. His siblings were also high achievers: Meredith's sister Dixie became a famous playwright, and his brother Cedric an innovator in the field of aggregate and concrete. The Willson Boyhood Home is open for tours.

Meredith Willson Boyhood Home, 314 S. Pennsylvania Ave. (formerly Superior Ave.), Mason City, IA 50401
(866) 228-6262 or (641) 424-2852
E-mail: mmsquare@mach3ww.com
Hours: May–October, daily 1–4 P.M.; November–April, Saturday–Sunday 1–5 P.M., or weekdays by appointment
Cost: Home, Adults $4, Kids (6–12) $2
www.themusicmansquare.org
Directions: One block east of Delaware Ave. (Rte. 65) at Second St. SE, then one block south on Pennsylvania Ave.

Willson never failed to fondly and shamelessly plug his hometown whenever he could. When *The Music Man* was made into a movie in 1962, it premiered at Mason City's Palace Theater with the entire cast in attendance. Arthur Godfrey was master of ceremonies.

For its part, Mason City has returned the affection. The town named the walkway over Willow Creek's Rock Glen Gorge the Meredith Willson Memorial Footbridge (Second Street SE and Connecticut Avenue). In 2002, Music Man Square opened adjacent to his birthplace. The complex's 1912 streetscape should look familiar—it was based on blueprints from the movie set. They've got Widow Paroo's front porch, the Reunion Hall, an ice cream parlor, and the Pleazol Billiard Parlor. The square also has a museum of band instruments and Willson memorabilia (including a flute played in the movie), as well as the Alan Bates Harmonica Collection.

Meredith Willson died in California on June 16, 1984. His body was returned to his hometown and was buried in Elmwood Cemetery (1224 S. Washington Avenue, (641) 421-3687). Ronald Reagan posthumously awarded Willson the Presidential Medal of Freedom in 1988.

Music Man Square and Meredith Willson Museum, 308 S. Pennsylvania Ave., Mason City, IA 50401

(866) 228-6262 or (641) 424-2852

E-mail: mmsquare@mach3ww.com

Hours: Daily 1–5 P.M.; Museum Tuesday–Sunday 1–5 P.M.

Cost: Square, Free; Museum, Adults $5, Kids (6–12) $2.50

www.themusicmansquare.org

Directions: Adjacent to the Meredith Willson Boyhood Home.

MASON CITY

When Mary Rogan, an employee at Mason City's Eureka House, expressed pleasure on learning of Abraham Lincoln's assassination, the good women of Mason City led her down to Willow Creek and tossed her in. Three times.

TROUBLE, RIGHT HERE IN MASON CITY

So, just how closely does Meredith Willson's River City compare to Mason City? Here are a few curious similarities:

★ The name River City was likely a reference to Willson's mother Rosalie's lifelong campaign to have Willow Creek and Lime Creek, which both run through town, renamed as rivers.

★ Marian the Librarian was almost certainly based on his mother. Rosalie was a progressive civic force, starting the county's first kindergarten and Mason City's first chapter of the Humane Society.

★ Willson also claimed a childhood friend, Charlie Haverdegraine, was the inspiration for Winthrop. But the young boy with the lisp was also inspired by an oft-repeated tale from his mother's Sunday School class. Asked what he would do first if he had spent 40 days and 40 nights in the desert, as Jesus had, the child responded, "Pith."

★ The school board's barbershop quartet, played by the Buffalo Bills, was fashioned after the Rusty Hinges, a Mason City group.

★ Henry Hill's Boys Band was based on a Mason City Boys Band organized by J. H. Jeffers. Both Meredith and his brother Cedric played in the band.

★ A November 24, 1916, edition of the Mason City *Globe-Gazette* had an article titled "Boys Must Keep Out of Billiard Establishments." It read, in part, " . . . it has become necessary for the proper authorities to take steps to curb the propensity of high school boys to play pool and billiards in the public pool halls, and some of the proprietors—in violation of the law—to let them." Sounds like trouble . . . with a capital T.

MASON CITY

John Dillinger's gang robbed the First National Bank of Mason City (now City Center, Federal Avenue at State Street) on March 13, 1934. The take was about $52,000. Dillinger was wounded in the heist, shot from an upper-floor bank window by Mason City Judge John Shipley.

Watch your head.
Photo by author, courtesy of Spook Cave.

McGregor
Spook Cave

Most folks would run the other way if they heard strange groaning noises coming from a hillside along a waterway dubbed Bloody Run Creek. But Gerald Mielke wasn't like most folks—he decided to check it out, and what he found is known today as Spook Cave.

Mielke widened the opening to the limestone cave, but not by much. The only way to visit Spook Cave today is to take the half-hour guided boat tour. The first 50 feet or so of your journey you must put your head between your knees to avoid getting beaned in the low passageway. Once you're back in the cave you can sit upright and appreciate the stalactites and the cool 47°F temperature. Eventually you find yourself wedged into the far reaches of the cave, where your guide starts relating stories of how the water level can change (for the worse!) in a thunderstorm. Did you check the weather reports before you embarked on this journey?

13299 Spook Cave Rd., McGregor, IA 52157

(563) 873-2144

E-mail: spookcave@spookcave.com

Hours: June–August, daily 9 A.M.–5:30 P.M.

Cost: Adults $8, Kids (4–12) $5

www.spookcave.com

Directions: Seven miles west of town on Rte. 18, then north on Spook Cave Rd. just east of Rte. 52.

New Hampton
Martha Timm Memorial Rock Garden

Martha Timm wasn't the type of woman who ever rested, not even in retirement. After raising a family on a farm southeast of New Hampton, she and her husband retired to town . . . and Martha got to work. Over the next several years she built an elaborate rock garden that included miniature churches, buildings, vases, birdbaths, and planters, all made from concrete and encrusted with stones and chips of broken glass and pottery. Timm also used at least one stone from every state in the union, either collected by her or her family and friends.

Timm passed away several years ago, and, rather than bulldoze the environment when her home was sold, the town rallied and moved her works to a park on the east side of town. Every community should have citizens that are this civic-minded.

Main St. and Fourth Ave., New Hampton, IA 50659

No phone

Hours: Always visible

Cost: Free

www.newhamptoniowa.com

Directions: Six blocks west of the railroad tracks on Rte. 24 (Main St.).

Newton
International Wrestling Institute and Museum

Everyone has heard of the world's oldest *profession*, but have you ever heard of the world's oldest *sport*? The Bible suggests that it was wrestling: a no-holds-barred match between Jacob and the Angel of the Lord. For the secular out there, you can also read a tale of wrestling in the *Epic of Gilgamesh*, the first-known book, written more than 5,000 years ago. Yes, wrestling can be traced back much further than the ancient Greek Olympics.

And it's still going strong, as evidenced by this popular museum. Owners Mike and Bev Chapman provided the seed artifacts for a collection that has grown to include Olympic medals, photos, singlets, trophies, films, antique wrestling cards, comic strips, books, training equipment, and a half-sized professional ring. They've even got a painting of a young, bare-chested Abe Lincoln settling a conflict the old-fashioned way, and it wasn't through debating or fancy-pants lawyering. Yes, Lincoln was a wrestler, and probably would have put Jefferson Davis in a choke-hold had he gotten his hands on that puny Reb!

Downstairs at the museum you'll find the Hall of Fame, where two new members are inducted each year. Read about wrestling legends like Dan Gable, Frank Gotch, Doug Blubaugh, Rulon Gardner, and more. And before you leave, don't forget to visit the gift shop.

1690 W. 19th St. S, PO Box 794, Newton, IA 50208

(641) 791-1517

E-mail: museum@pcpartner.net

Hours: Tuesday–Saturday 10 A.M.–5 P.M.

Cost: Adults $5, Kids (6–17) $3

www.wrestlingmuseum.org

Directions: North on Rte. 6/14 from I-80, left on S. 12th Ave. W, then south on W. 19th St. S.

NEVADA

Evangelist **Billy Sunday** was born near Nevada on November 19, 1862.

In 1996 a Nevada farmer found a 30-foot-diameter crop circle in his bean field.

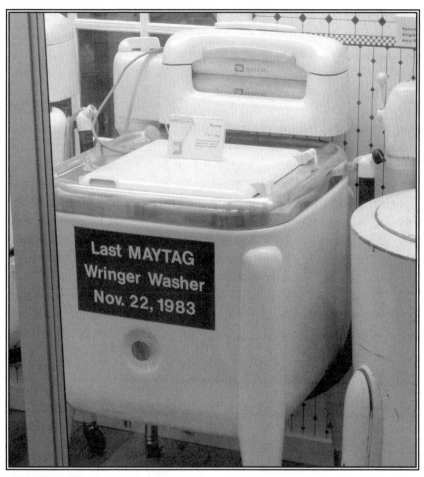

Good riddance.
Photo by author, courtesy of Jasper County Museum.

Maytag Historical Center

What would your life be like if you had to wash all your clothes by hand? Well, you never have to imagine such a horror now, thanks in no small part to Howard Snyder and Fred Maytag.

The story begins in the 1890s when Newton inventor Arthur Ogburn came up with the first primitive washing machine, a hand-cranked device called the Ratchet Slat. Local manufacturer Fred Maytag specialized in farm equipment, but he wasn't above taking chances in other areas. One of his employees, engineer Howard Snyder, came up with his own version of Ogburn's washing machine in 1907, which Maytag named the Pastime. Two years later Snyder added a gasoline-powered belt drive to the clothing agitator, and the Hired Girl model was born. In 1911 the first electric model—the Maytag Power Washer—hit the appliance showroom, and the modern washing machine was born.

You'll be able to trace the entire history of the Maytag Corporation on the second floor of this fantastic small town museum. You'll learn how, over the years, Maytag added other features to assist the homemaker; some later models would grind meat, churn butter, or make ice cream at the same time they were agitating undies. The museum has the 25 millionth washer Maytag ever built, as well as the last wringer model ever to roll off the assembly line... on November 22, *1983*! Any wonder why they never sold it?

There was a time when Newton was home to nine different washing machine manufacturers, but now Maytag is the only one left. The town still calls itself the Washing Machine Center of the World.

Jasper County Historical Museum, 1700 S. 15th Ave. W, PO Box 834, Newton, IA 50208

(641) 792-9118

E-mail: jascomus@pcpartner.net

Hours: May–September, daily 1–5 P.M.

Cost: Adults $3, Kids $1

www.jaspercountymuseum.org

Directions: Head north from I-80 on Rte. 14/6, turn right on 12th Ave. W, then south on the first right onto 15th Ave. W.

OTHER IOWA HOUSEHOLD INVENTIONS

★ In 1934, after struggling to unclog his daughter's toilet—she had been unsuccessfully flushing potato peels—Sam Blanc of Des Moines came up with the **Roto-Rooter** by attaching a Maytag washing machine motor to an auger "snake." Today there's a Roto-Rooter Hall of Fame (www.rotorooter.com) at the company headquarters in West Des Moines.

★ In August 1967, the **Radarange**, the first commercial microwave oven, was introduced to the American public. The technology had been developed in 1945 by Dr. Percy Spencer of the Raytheon Corporation, a subsidiary of Amana Refrigeration of Newton. The Iowa-based company launched its $495 model two decades later.

Beware the Thirteen Steps. . . .

Palo
The Thirteen Steps

Thirteen is said to be an unlucky number, so it probably comes as little surprise that the Pleasant Ridge Cemetery, accessed by a flight of thirteen steps, is a particularly unlucky graveyard. Many visitors claim the cemetery is guarded by a phantom dog atop the highest step. Others have spotted balls of green light dancing on the graves of the Lewis family. And there have also been reports of a ghost house that materializes in an adjacent grassy clearing.

Which story should you believe? Probably none of them. But that doesn't mean you shouldn't repeat these stories to in order to frighten your friends when you visit this graveyard. Of course you should—that's the whole point of listening to ghost stories.

Pleasant Ridge Cemetery, Palo Marsh Rd., Palo, IA 52324

No phone

Hours: Always visible

Cost: Free

Directions: Head north from town two miles on Rte. W36 (Palo Marsh Rd.); the cemetery is on a hillside on the left side of the road, on the east side of Pleasant Creek State Park.

Gary Busey, in deer form.

St. Ansgar
Albino Deer

In the spring of 1980 folks around St. Ansgar first began seeing a snow-white fawn. The reports checked out, though it wasn't the ghost of a pure-of-heart Indian maiden. No, just a female albino whitetail. Over the next eight years she wandered the countryside north of town, never straying more than five miles from where she was born, and never being dropped by a hunter. She gave birth to 15 fawns, none of which were albinos.

On December 13, 1988, the white deer died of pneumonia, kidney failure, and old age. Locals found her body and had it mounted for future generations to admire. You can see her any time of day or night in a glassed pavilion in St. Ansgar's business district, staring out at visitors with her creepy pink eyes.

White Deer Park, Fourth and Mitchell Sts., St. Ansgar, IA 50472

(641) 713-4921

Hours: Always visible

Cost: Free

www.stansgar.org

Directions: Downtown on Fourth St., three blocks west of the railroad tracks.

Spillville
The Bily Clocks

Winters in Iowa can be long and cold, and if you're a bachelor farmer, you've got a lot of time on your hands. Brothers Joseph and Frank Bily put their time to good use building 42 intricately carved clocks between 1913 and 1958. Joseph designed the clocks and Frank carved the pieces. Though some are small, many are taller than the average human. Their names reflect the scenes portrayed on them, such as the History of the United States, the book of Genesis, the Parade of Nations, the Twelve Apostles (with gargoyles!), the History of Travel, and Lindbergh's Transatlantic Flight.

As far-reaching as their clocks' themes could be, the Bilys weren't exactly worldly men; neither traveled more than 35 miles from Spillville in their entire lives. When Mr. Bigshot Henry Ford showed up at their door in 1928 and offered them $1 million for the Pioneer Clock, the brothers turned him down cold—they weren't particularly interested in money. Though they charged visitors 10¢ each to see the clocks in their later years, they never cashed in the dimes; instead, they hid the coins beneath the floorboards of their home.

In their old age the Bilys contemplated having the clocks burned upon their deaths, but the town of Spillville convinced them to donate the masterpieces for posterity, which is why you can still see them today. Whatever you do, don't reset your wristwatch to the museum's clocks. They're not malfunctioning; they're set out of sync so they don't chime, ring, and gong all at the same moment.

Bily Clock Museum, 323 S. Main St., PO Box 258, Spillville, IA 52168

(563) 562-3569

E-mail: bilyclocks@oneota.net

Hours: May–October, daily 8:30 A.M.–5 P.M.; April, daily 10 A.M.–4 P.M.; March and November, Saturday–Sunday 10 A.M.–4 P.M.

Cost: Adults $4.50, Seniors (65+) $4, Kids (7–18) $3

www.bilyclocks.org

Directions: Two blocks north of Rte. 325 (Victory St.) on Main St.

ANTONÍN DVOŘÁK SLEPT HERE

Composer **Antonín Dvořák** needed to get away from the city to think. Being Czech, he decided to go someplace where they spoke his language, and Spillville was that place. So in the summer of 1893 he packed his bags, left the New York Conservatory of Music, and headed for Iowa. While staying in the building that today houses the Bily Clock Museum, he completed his Ninth Symphony, "From the New World," and wrote the Quintet in E-flat and the String Quartet in F, sometimes known as the "American Quartette." On Sundays he played the organ at the St. Wenceslaus Church (on Church Street). You can see some Dvořák memorabilia upstairs at the Bily Clock Museum or attend Spillville's International Dvořák Festival, held every year on the first weekend in August.

PLYMOUTH

Plymouth is named for a rock along the Shell Rock River. It reminded the town's founders of Plymouth Rock.

PRINCETON

William Frederick Cody, best known as **Buffalo Bill**, was born near Princeton on February 26, 1846. After his older brother Sam was killed in a riding accident in 1852, Cody's family sold its homestead, Napsinekee Place, and moved to Kansas. The cabin burned down years ago, but a re-creation now stands on the site (28050 230th Avenue, (563) 225-2981).

Berry big.

Strawberry Point
World's Largest Strawberry

When you live in a town named Strawberry Point, how might you attract tourists? Build the World's Largest Cantaloupe? No, that would only lead to confusion. But a supersized strawberry? That's the ticket!

Strawberry Point's big-ass berry was erected in the late 1960s. It measures 15 feet from top to bottom and is impaled on a giant spike outside City Hall. The strawberry is covered in bright yellow seeds, which, if planted, might produce enough fiberglass fruit to feed an army.

As if this monument wasn't enough, Strawberry Point also celebrates Strawberry Days on the second weekend in June. The highlight of the day includes free ice cream, topped with sweet, juicy cantaloupe. Excuse me, *strawberries*.

City Hall, 111 Commercial St., Strawberry Point, IA 52076

(563) 933-4417

Hours: Always visible

Cost: Free

www.strawberrypt.com/cityhal.htm

Directions: One block south of Rte. 3 (Mission St.) on Rte. 13 (Commercial St.).

SABULA
Sabula is the only town in Iowa located on an island.

STRAWBERRY POINT
A lamp from the movie *Gone with the Wind* is on display at the Wilder Memorial Museum (123 W. Mission Street, (563) 933-4615) in Strawberry Point.

STATE CENTER
State Center has proclaimed itself the Rose Capitol of Iowa.

Just in case you get lost.

Tama
Lincoln Highway Bridge

The coast-to-coast route of the Lincoln Highway (U.S. 30) has changed often since it was first laid out in 1913. As towns along the road grew, the Lincoln Highway was often rerouted to new, wider streets that bypassed downtown districts. Today the only way to find the true original route is to consult a guidebook.

Not so in Tama. If you want to know where the Lincoln Highway came though town, just look for the bridge on Fifth Street, which was built in 1915. The vertical concrete joists holding up the bridge railing spell out "LINCOLN HIGHWAY" in capital letters. You'd think every town on the

Main Street of America would want a bridge like this, but there is only one other bridge like it between New York and San Francisco, and it's in Nevada.

E. Fifth St. (old Lincoln Highway), Tama, IA 52339

(641) 484-6661

Hours: Always visible

Cost: Free

www.tamatoledo.com

Directions: On Fifth St. at Taylor Dr. on the east side of town, just west of the Tama
 Florist.

Traer
The Winding Stairs

E. E. Taylor, founder of the Traer *Star-Clipper*, wanted a little more room in his 18-foot-wide newspaper office, so in 1894 he decided to move his building's stairs out onto the street. Like some sort of *Trading Spaces* redecorating nightmare, Taylor had a spiral staircase attached to the Second Street facade and opened a door on the second floor. Anyone wanting to visit the paper had to climb its 23 steps. If it was snowing or raining, too bad.

Then, in 1916, Traer decided to widen its downtown sidewalks. Rather than scrap his unique entryway, Taylor just moved the staircase out to the new curb and built a catwalk connecting the upper door to the top step. The structure looked a little wacky, but it served its purpose.

Today the Winding Stairs are listed on the National Register of Historic Places, and the folks of Traer throw a Winding Stairs Festival on the third weekend in August each year.

Second St., Traer, IA 50675

(319) 478-2346

Hours: Always visible

Cost: Free

www.traer.com/visit/winding_stairs.html

Directions: One block west of Main St. (Rte. 63) on Second St.

Waterloo
Sullivan Memorial Park

When brothers George, Francis, Joseph, Madison, and Albert Sullivan learned that their friend Bill Ball (of nearby Fredericksburg) had been killed aboard the USS *Arizona* at Pearl Harbor, they decided to enlist in the U.S. Navy. Together. Against the advice of several officers, the navy agreed to their terms, and the fivesome was assigned to the USS *Juneau*, headed for the South Pacific. Sadly, the light cruiser was lost in the battle for Guadalcanal on November 13, 1942. Of the 687 crew, only 11 men survived to return home. Of the Sullivans, only George made it to a lifeboat before the ship sank. He died several days later while waiting to be rescued; he had gotten out of the lifeboat to "take a bath" and was attacked by a shark.

The tragedy spurred the U.S. Congress to write a bill revising navy policy to prevent multiple family members from serving on the same ship. It seemed like a good idea, but the proposed legislation never passed. Though the Congress and military had second thoughts, the Sullivan family (who lived at 98 Adams Street) apparently did not; the brothers' only sister, Genevieve, enlisted in the WAVES after learning of their deaths. Genevieve lived to see the end of the war and a memorial park in her hometown dedicated to her brave family and its tremendous sacrifice. Part of the park sits atop the old Sullivan homesite. Waterloo has renamed its convention center the Five Sullivan Brothers Convention Center.

Ankeny and Adams Sts., Waterloo, IA 50703

No phone

Hours: Always visible

Cost: Free

www.wplwloo.lib.ia.us/sullivanbrothers.html

Directions: Two blocks east of Mullan Ave. (Rte. 63), three blocks south of Newell St.

WATERLOO

Rumors have long circulated that a gambler buried $15,000 near a filling station south of Waterloo, then died in an auto wreck. It has never been recovered.

WAVERLY

A UFO reportedly hovered over the Red Fox Inn in Waverly on September 15, 1996. It then followed two patrons while they drove to a convenience store.

Wild west Godzilli.

Waukon
Cowboy and Steer

Iowa isn't exactly the wild, wild west, but you wouldn't know it if you visit a feed store at the south end of Waukon. A 15-foot cowboy looms over Village Farm & Home, flanked by an equally massive steer who's scraping his front hoof against the soil, ready to charge. The cowboy is decked out in a red shirt, blue jeans, and a 800-gallon hat. The steer wears nothing at all.

Village Farm & Home, 1718 Rossville Rd., Waukon, IA 52172

(563) 568-4577

Hours: Always visible

Cost: Free

Directions: South of town on Rte. 76 (Rossville Rd.), just north of the Rte. 9 intersection.

West Branch
Herbert Hoover Presidential Library

Herbert Hoover was born in West Branch on August 10, 1874, the son of a Quaker blacksmith, but before the age of nine he was an orphan. He was quickly packed up and shipped to Oregon, where he spent the rest of his childhood with his uncle.

His trauma-filled youth didn't seem to slow him down much. After successful careers as an engineer and a civil servant, he became the first U.S. president born west of the Mississippi. In his 1928 presidential campaign he promised "A chicken in every pot and a car in every garage." Within a year of his inauguration, however, many Americans had neither pots nor garages—the stock market crashed on October 29, 1929.

In a magnanimous gesture, Hoover never accepted a salary as president. That's not to say he was a man of the people; while living in the White House, the Hoovers demanded that all servants disappear if they heard the first couple coming, which was announced by a special bell.

Don't expect the folks at this presidential library to dwell too long on Black Tuesday, though. They want to tell you about how Hoover received worldwide acclaim as director of food aid after World War I. He was also responsible for standardizing the milk bottle. But blame him for the Great Depression? Try *your* hand at the computer simulation to see if you can stop the inevitable economic downturn, Mr. or Ms. Smartypants!

When Hoover died on October 20, 1964, he was interred here. His wife, Lou Henry, who had preceded him in death, was exhumed from her California grave and moved to Iowa. The folks of West Branch have let Depression bygones be bygones, and now host Hoover Fest here each August.

Herbert Hoover National Historic Site, 234 S. Downey St., PO Box 607, West Branch, IA 52358

(319) 643-2541

Hours: Daily 9 A.M.–5 P.M.

Cost: Adults $4, Kids (under 16) Free

www.nps.gov/heho

Directions: At the corner of Parkside Dr. and Main St.

Herbert H. Hoover Presidential Library–Museum, 110 Parkside Dr., PO Box 488, West Branch, IA 52358

(319) 643-5301

Hours: Daily 9 A.M.–5 P.M.

Cost: Adults $4, Seniors (62+) $2, Kids (under 17) Free

www.hoover.archives.gov

Directions: Two blocks south of Main St. on Parkside Dr.

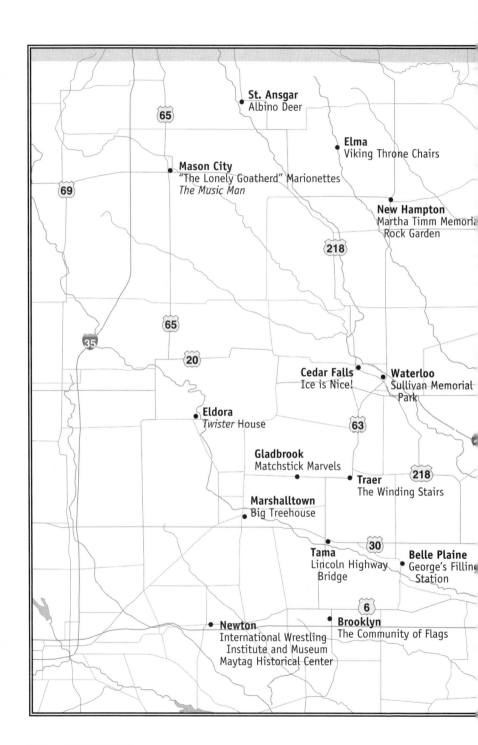

St. Ansgar
Albino Deer

65

Elma
Viking Throne Chairs

Mason City
"The Lonely Goatherd" Marionettes
The Music Man

69

New Hampton
Martha Timm Memoria
Rock Garden

218

65

35

20

Cedar Falls
Ice is Nice!

Waterloo
Sullivan Memorial
Park

Eldora
Twister House

63

Gladbrook
Matchstick Marvels

Traer
The Winding Stairs

218

Marshalltown
Big Treehouse

Tama
Lincoln Highway
Bridge

30

Belle Plaine
George's Filling
Station

6

Newton
International Wrestling
Institute and Museum
Maytag Historical Center

Brooklyn
The Community of Flags

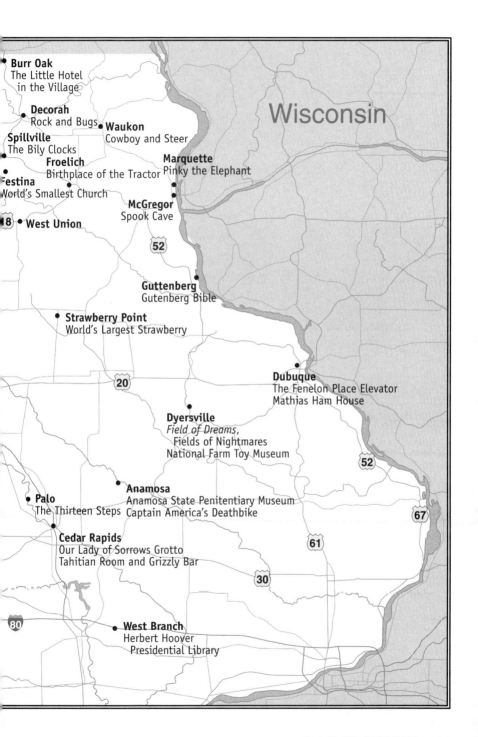

Burr Oak
The Little Hotel
in the Village

Decorah
Rock and Bugs **Waukon**
Cowboy and Steer
Spillville
The Bily Clocks
Froelich **Marquette**
Birthplace of the Tractor Pinky the Elephant
Festina
World's Smallest Church
McGregor
Spook Cave
(18) **West Union**

Wisconsin

(52)

Guttenberg
Gutenberg Bible

Strawberry Point
World's Largest Strawberry

(20)

Dubuque
The Fenelon Place Elevator
Mathias Ham House

Dyersville
Field of Dreams,
Fields of Nightmares
National Farm Toy Museum

(52)

Anamosa
Anamosa State Penitentiary Museum
Palo Captain America's Deathbike
The Thirteen Steps

(67)

Cedar Rapids
Our Lady of Sorrows Grotto
Tahitian Room and Grizzly Bar

(61)

(30)

(80)

West Branch
Herbert Hoover
Presidential Library

3

THE SOUTHWEST

Considering the relatively sparse population in this corner of Iowa, the southwest has produced an impressive list of celebrities. It's the birthplace of the king of late-night television, the world's most popular apple, the best-known actor in movie westerns, and the queen of coffee pushers (pre-Starbucks). No wonder the Iowa Walk of Fame is located in Shenandoah!

But the stories of southwest Iowa are not all fame and fortune. Did you know that America's largest ax murder—in terms of victims—took place in southwest Iowa? And that the eight murders are still *unsolved*? Hmmmm . . . better double-check the deadbolt on your motel door. . . .

Clarinda
Birthplace of 4-H

Educator Jesse Field believed the Three Rs weren't nearly enough, so she added Three Hs: Head, Heart, and Hands. It wasn't that her students at the Goldenrod School didn't have all of these body parts; they just didn't seem to use them. So in 1901 she formed the Boys' Corn Club to teach them about seed selection, livestock judging, and other farming skills. A Girls' Home Club was also organized, but with domestic concerns in mind: sewing, baking, and tending to a garden. The clubs were a hit.

By 1906, Field was married—now she was Jesse Field Shambaugh—and superintendent of the Page County school district. In 1907, O. H. Benson of Clarion designed the now familiar 4-H emblem, though it only had three Hs at the time. Shambaugh later added a fourth H leaf, for Home, which was later changed to Health to stay with the times. You can still see Field's former one-room schoolhouse where this spunky teacher first launched her big idea.

Goldenrod School, Nodaway Valley Museum, 1600 S. 16th St., Clarinda, IA 51632

(712) 542-3073

Hours: May–October, Tuesday–Sunday 1–5 P.M.; November–April, Tuesday–Sunday 2–4 P.M., or by appointment

Cost: Adults $2, Kids (12 and under) Free

www.clarinda.org/4-H.htm

Directions: One block south of Rte. 2 on Glenn Miller Ave. (Rte. 71), at the south end of town.

Birthplace of Glenn Miller

Glenn Miller was born in Clarinda on March 1, 1904, and though he didn't live here very long—his family moved away in 1908—the town has never forgotten him. The National Guard armory in Clarinda (701 W. Washington Street) was renamed the Glenn Miller Armory in 1954. The annual International Glenn Miller Festival is held here on the second weekend each June, with the proceeds going toward a future Glenn Miller Museum.

The Glenn Miller Historical Society hopes to build the museum behind the bandleader's Clarinda birthplace. Until then, you can see the town's Millerabilia in his former home, including one of his four trombones and the golden record for "Chattanooga Choo Choo." And you'll learn all about his brief but impressive career, cut short on December 15, 1944, when his plane disappeared over the English Channel.

601 S. 16th St., Clarinda, IA 51632

Contact: Glenn Miller Historical Society, 107 E. Main St., Clarinda, IA 51632

(712) 542-2461

E-mail: gmbs@heartland.net

Hours: May–September, Tuesday–Sunday 1–5 P.M.; October–April, Tuesday–Sunday 2–4 P.M.

Cost: Free

www.glennmiller.org

Directions: Six blocks north of Rte. 2 on Glenn Miller Ave. (16th St.), at Clark St.

Corning
Birthplace of Johnny Carson

From all his talk about Norfolk, Nebraska, you'd think Johnny Carson was born there. Not so. He entered the world in Corning, Iowa, on October 23, 1925. Carson's father was the area manager for the Iowa–Nebraska Power & Light Company, which meant the family had to move often. While Johnny was still an infant, the Carsons moved to Clarinda, and shortly thereafter to Red Oak.

While living in Red Oak, he started taking a correspondence course in ventriloquism, which spurred his interest in magic. Before he could use his creepy new skills, the family moved again, this time to Avoca. There, on the front porch of 725 Cherry Street, Carson first entertained an audience of his peers. Local kids gathered to see the Great Carsoni, and they were not disappointed. Neither was Carson; he'd been infected with the show business bug. The Carsons soon moved to Nebraska, where the teenage Great Carsoni landed his first paying gig at Norfolk's Granada Theatre.

500 13th St., Corning, IA 50841

Private phone

Hours: Always visible; view from street

Cost: Free

www.johnnycarson.com

Directions: Two blocks west of Happy Hollow Rd. (Rte. 148) at Davis Ave.

Beware, thirsty visitors!

Council Bluffs
The Angel of Death and Bloomers

In 1916 Ruth Anne Dodge, widow of railroad pioneer General Grenville
Dodge, started having a recurring dream: a winged angel on the prow of

a boat sailed up to Dodge and offered her something to quench her thirst. "Drink; I bring you both a promise and a blessing," the angel implored. The dream repeated three nights in a row, and on the third visit Ruth Anne took the angel up on her offer. The next morning, Ruth Anne's daughters noticed that their mother awoke with a sense of calm, and by the end of the day was even calmer. She was dead.

Holding no grudge against the angel, Ruth Anne's daughters commissioned a sculpture from Daniel Chester French, the man who would one day sculpt the Lincoln Memorial in Washington, D.C. The Ruth Anne Dodge Memorial, often called the Black Angel or the Angel of Death, beckons Fairview Cemetery visitors with a flowing vessel of impending death to this day. I recommend you bring bottled water. Local legend claims that the spooky bronze lifts from its base and flies around the cemetery at night.

On your visit to Fairview, you can also visit the grave of Amelia Jenks Bloomer, who died on December 30, 1894. An editor and suffragist, Bloomer advocated temperance, abolition, and women's rights. However, she is best remembered for the fashion item that bears her name: bloomers. Invented in the 1850s by Elizabeth Smith Miller, the Turkish pantaloons became popular with female bicyclists and others who wanted to be free of cumbersome ankle-length dresses. They were eventually nicknamed bloomers after their biggest advocate. Bloomer lived in Council Bluffs at 123 Fourth Street with her husband Dexter. (Their home has since been torn down.)

Fairview Cemetery, N. Second and Lafayette Ave., Council Bluffs, IA 51503

(712) 328-4992

Hours: Daylight hours

Cost: Free

Directions: Seven block north of Pierce St. (Rte. 6) on Second St.

CORNING
It is a misdemeanor in Corning for a man to ask his wife to ride in an automobile.

The Big Lake Incident

Something fell from the sky over Council Bluffs on December 17, 1977, and *it's still there!* Witnesses followed the large object as it slammed into a dike running through Big Lake Park, shooting flames 10 feet into the air. Glowing, molten metal was scattered around the point of impact, and the vaporized water fell back on the crater as snow.

Metallurgists examined the composition of the fragments, and ruled out that it was a meteorite. The mystery was reported over the AP wire, but nobody came forward with an explanation. What was it? Maybe you can find out for yourself; a large chunk of whatever it was is still beneath the water's surface at Big Lake.

Big Lake Park, 2600 N. Eighth St., Council Bluffs, IA 51503

(712) 328-4650

Hours: Always visible

Cost: Free

http://parksandrec.councilbluffs-ia.gov/parks.asp

Directions: Head north on Rte. 192 (16 St.), then right on Big Lake Rd. just before the I-29 interchange, on the north end of town.

God's Wrath

Henry DeLong was a gambler at the tender age of seven. His favorite betting parlor was the Ocean Wave Saloon in Council Bluffs, back when it was still a frontier town. But in 1858 DeLong took a long, hard look at his own devilish behavior and swore off his childhood vices. He must have been relieved when, three years later, God struck the Ocean Wave with a bolt of lightning. The den of sin quickly burned to the ground.

During the Civil War, DeLong washed shirts at 5¢ a pop and managed to save enough money to eventually purchase the land where the Ocean Wave once stood. He donated it to a local congregation to build a new church: Broadway United Methodist. Whether you believe a higher power was involved in this story, or that it was just bum luck, the folks at Broadway United Methodist accept the former. They even erected a plaque out front to celebrate their good fortune. The sign is no longer there, but the church is, and its members will be glad to tell you all about DeLong's weather-endorsed conversion.

Broadway United Methodist Church, 11 S. First St., Cedar Rapids, IA 51503

(712) 322-7741

Hours: Always visible

Cost: Free

www.rootsweb.com/~iapottaw/chCBBdwyUMC.html

Directions: At the corner of First St. and Rte. 6 (Pierce St.).

GOD WORKS IN MYSTERIOUS WAYS

Before you draw too broad a conclusion about God's intentions from the burning of the Ocean Wave Saloon, look to southeast Iowa and the Sts. Peter and Paul Church Cemetery near Harper (30832 242nd Street). During a 1991 thunderstorm a bolt of lightning struck the graveyard's main crucifix . . . and Jesus *exploded*!

A similar fate met Steamboat Rock in the town of (no surprise) Steamboat Rock. The town's namesake geologic formation disintegrated in 1885 when lightning struck a tree whose roots had burrowed into the rock. Water in the roots vaporized, shattering the stone around them. Today folks ask, "Why do they call this town Steamboat Rock?" and all they can point to is a pile of rubble.

And finally, in the 1850s, lightning struck a cross at the Old Mission church near Festina (see page 81). The congregation started attending another church. Pronto.

CRESTON

Marcia Wallace, Carol on *The Bob Newhart Show* and Miss Krabapple on *The Simpsons*, was born in Creston on November 1, 1942.

Creston sits atop a crest that separates the Mississippi and Missouri River watersheds, hence its name.

Is that your eastern terminus, or are you just happy to see me?

The Golden Spike

In 1859, soon-to-be–Civil War General Grenville Dodge took soon-to-be-president Abraham Lincoln to a spot on the bluffs overlooking the Missouri River and explained his vision: a transcontinental railroad linking east and west. Since Council Bluffs was already connected via rail to the East Coast, the railroad would start in Dodge's new hometown. Lincoln took Dodge's advice, and in 1865 Council Bluffs was named the eastern terminus of the massive project. Sacramento was chosen as the western terminus, and the Union Pacific Railroad was created to lay the tracks.

Lincoln didn't live long enough to see the route become a reality, but the folks here never forgot the favor. In 1911 a granite shaft was erected on the spot where Lincoln once stood (Lafayette Avenue and N. Seventh Street). And in 1939, to celebrate the premiere of the movie *Union Pacific*, the city unveiled a 56-foot golden spike, similar to the one pounded at Promontory Point, Utah, on May 10, 1869. Council Bluffs's spike may not be made of gold (it's concrete), but it's a hell of a lot bigger, and isn't that what matters most?

Golden Spike Monument, 9th Ave. and 21st St., Council Bluffs, IA 51501

No phone

Hours: Always visible

Cost: Free

Directions: Seven blocks south of Second Ave., four blocks east of 25th St.

Squirrel Cage Jail

Act like a rat and the cops will treat you like a rodent. A squirrel, to be precise . . . at least in Council Bluffs. From 1885 to 1969, local scofflaws cooled their heels in this city's unique rotary jail. Shaped like an oversized coffee can, the Pottawattamie County Jail stands three stories tall with ten two-prisoner cells per level. To enter or exit a cell, the warden would rotate the entire cellblock until one interior door aligned with a single door on the outside frame. This design discouraged massive jailbreaks. In fact, only eleven men ever escaped during its 84 years of service, and they all escaped after modifications were made to the original configuration. The building was ruled a fire hazard because the inmates couldn't be quickly rescued if the structure ever started burning, so the rotary mechanism was cemented in place and additional doors were cut into the outer cage.

The jail was very noisy—mostly because of the prisoners—and the neighbors started to complain. In 1969 a new jail opened its soon-to-be-locked doors and this hoosegow got the heave-ho. Because it was one of only three "squirrel cage" jails ever built, locals preserved the building and opened it to the public. In addition to the main cellblock, the current museum has displays on famous inmates, the warden's family quarters, and the female cell block.

Ghost hunters will be interested to know that the jail is said to be haunted by a wispy figure. Most think it is the spirit of J. M. Carter, the building's first superintendent, but others think it may be the ghost of one of only two men to have ever died here. The first suffered a heart attack. The other dashed his brains out on the floor; he was scratching his initials when he fell from a ceiling beam. That'll teach him to vandalize!

Pottawattamie County Jail, 226 Pearl St., Council Bluffs, IA 51503

Contact: PO Box 2, Council Bluffs, IA 51502

(712) 323-2509

Hours: May and September, Saturday–Sunday Noon–4 P.M.; June–August,
  Wednesday–Saturday 10 A.M.–4 P.M., Sunday Noon–4 P.M.

Cost: Adults $5, Seniors $4, Kids (6–12) $4

www.geocities.com/heartland/plains/5660/sqcgjail.htm

Directions: Downtown between First and Willow Sts., one block east of Sixth St.
  (Rte. 192), two blocks south of Broadway (Rte. 6).

BLACK SQUIRREL TOWN

Council Bluffs is overrun with black squirrels, and the folk here love it! They've even made these unique rodents their town's mascot. (Most American squirrels are brown or gray squirrels.) In 1975 the city council passed a law making it illegal to "annoy, worry, maim, injure, or kill a black squirrel" within city limits. The highest concentration of these curious critters can be found downtown in Bayliss Park, bounded by Sixth Street, First Avenue, Pearl Street, and Willow Avenue. And in case you're wondering, the selection of the town's squirrel cage-shaped jail has nothing to do with the local rodent population.

It's not a dollhouse.

Teeny Tiny House

McMansions, SUVs, supersized fast food—the motto in America today seems to be "bigger is better." That hasn't always been the case, particularly for those of diminutive stature. Jean and Inez Bregant operated an average-sized grocery store in Council Bluffs, but their home downtown was more to their liking. It was *dinky*. You see, Jean was 47 inches tall and weighed 66 pounds, while Inez was 45 inches tall and weighed 41 pounds. Their tiny home was built with low windows, light switches, sinks, and counters to accommodate them but decorated with standard furniture so they could entertain their friends.

The Bregants met while working for a Coney Island sideshow. Jean, who was born in Austria in 1869, was eighteen years older than Inez. Nevertheless, they fell in love and moved back to Inez's hometown of Council Bluffs where they were married on December 25, 1905. They opened a grocery on North Eighth Street and acted as spokespersons for a local confectionary, Woodward's Candy Company. Jean died at age 75 in 1944, but Inez lived to age 82, passing away in 1969. Their small home, while not open to the public, is still visible from the street.

517 Fourth St., Council Bluffs, IA 51503

Private phone

Hours: Always visible, view from street

Cost: Free

Directions: One block east of Main St., three blocks south of Broadway (Rte. 6).

World's Oldest Dairy Queen

While you might think your grungy hometown Dairy Queen has to be the oldest on the planet, the DQ on Broadway in Council Bluffs wants to set the record straight: it is. The proof is engraved on a plaque on the wall. This particular franchise was erected in 1946—the tenth ever—and is the world's oldest surviving DQ. But have no fear, while the structure may be 60 years old, the burgers and dip cones are not.

1634 W. Broadway, Council Bluffs, IA 51501

(712) 322-8801

Hours: Daily Noon–10:30 P.M.

Cost: Free; food extra

Directions: Just west of the Broadway viaduct at 17th St.

HAMBURG

Hamburg claims to be the Peony Capital of the World.

Crescent

Archer Engines of Yesteryear

Are you one of those folks who just can't throw away an old lawn mower, always thinking, hoping, praying, "Heck, I could get this running again"? Are you the type that buys other folks' lawn mowers at garage sales for $5, rationalizing, "I could use it for spare parts"? And do you cruise the alleys on trash day, searching for a Toro that somebody had thrown out, promising yourself, "I could rebuild it some weekend"? If you're that type, you'll feel right at home talking with Fred Archer, founder of Archer Engines of Yesteryear.

Archer has been collecting discarded mowers for years and has assembled an impressive collection dating back to 1890. Who even knew folks grew lawns back then? He's got everything from a century-old reel model to a modern Flymo, a Jetson-esque mowing hovercraft. Each mower has a story, if you're willing to ask. If you're more interested in chain saws than lawn mowers, Archer has a large sampling of them, too.

202 Riordon St., Crescent, IA 51526

(712) 545-3791

Hours: May–October, Monday–Saturday 10 A.M.–4:30 P.M., or by appointment

Cost: Free

Directions: At the north end of town, one block east of Rte. 183 (Old Lincoln Hwy.).

Creston

Frank Phillips Tourism Information Center

Frank Phillips, the founder of Phillips 66, originally wanted to be a barber. Why? He liked the striped pants barbers wore. Honestly. While growing up in Creston, Phillips admired the local barber's spiffy uniform and eventually became his apprentice. Having learned a skill, Phillips headed for the Utah silver fields in 1893. Two years later he returned to Creston and bought a barber shop at Montgomery and Pine streets. He fell in love with a banker's daughter and planned to ask for her hand in marriage, but was forced to sell his business to gain her father's approval. He wanted Phillips to enter a more "respectable" line of work. Specifically, banking.

Phillips worked for his father-in-law's institution until 1903, when Phillips moved his family to Oklahoma, which happened to be in the midst of an oil boom. Phillips founded the Citizens Bank and Trust of Bartlesville and used his profits to establish the Phillips Petroleum Corporation in 1917, partnering with his brother Frank. It would later become Phillips 66.

In 1931, Phillips 66 built one of Iowa's first gas stations at the corner of Route 34 and Cherry Street in his old hometown of Creston. In 1994 it was moved to the south end of town and restored. Today it serves as the county's tourism office. The historic building also houses a mini-museum of Phillips 66 artifacts.

Union County Tourism and Information Center, 636 New York Ave., PO Box 471, Creston, IA 50801

(641) 782-4405 or (641) 782-7021

E-mail: chamber@mddc.com

Hours: May–October, Monday–Saturday 8:30 A.M.–5 P.M.

Cost: Free

www.mddc.com/uct

Directions: Two blocks southwest of Sumner Ave. on Rte. 34 (New York Ave.), at Park St.

LENOX
Twenty-four inches of snow fell on Lenox on April 20, 1918, a one-day record for Iowa.

NODAWAY
The name Nodaway is derived from *nodawa*, a Native American term meaning "crossed without a canoe."

RED OAK
During World War II the town of Red Oak suffered more casualties, per capita, than any other city in the nation.

The dates are for the town, not the apple.

East Peru
Birthplace of the Delicious Apple

Not all apples come from Washington state. The Delicious apple, for example, was discovered by Jesse Hiatt in 1894, right here in East Peru (which was just Peru at the time). Though Hiatt had bred other apple varieties—the Hiatt Black and the Hiatt Sweet—the Delicious turned out to be just a stroke of dumb luck. One of his Bellflower apple trees was struck by lightning in 1872; the tree died, but a sapling came up from one of its roots. The little tree was growing between two rows so, infused with an Iowan's sense of orderliness, Hiatt chopped it down.

But the sapling grew back. Hiatt admired the plucky tree, and allowed it to grow this time. Ten years later, in 1883, it produced its first crop: a single apple. Hiatt thought it was *delicious*. He named it the Hawkeye, though, in honor of his home state. It was another decade before the tree grew to a size where it was producing enough fruit to enter into competition. Hiatt sent a bushel of Hawkeyes to the 1894 Missouri State Fair where they caught the attention of Clarence M. Stark, who purchased the propagation rights. Stark also gave it a new name: Delicious.

Ironic, eh? Is it just me, or is the Delicious apple the least delicious apple on the market? Anyway, there have been more than 15 million trees propagated from that first scrappy sapling. Though the original tree died some years ago, a new tree sprang from its roots. It is located on private land just off Hiatt Apple Road north of town but is not accessible to the general public. Apple fanatics have to content themselves with a historic marker at the center of town.

Emerson St., East Peru, IA 50273

No phone

Hours: Always visible

Cost: Free

Directions: Marker at the intersection of Rte. G68 (Emerson St.), and G8P (Odell Ave.).

Contact: Original Red Delicious Apples, 1210 Normal St., Woodbine, IA 51579

(712) 617-2520

www.original-red-delicious.com

Macksburg
National Skillet Throw

In order to salute its local women, the town of Macksburg began hosting the National Skillet Throw each June. The goal of the Skillet Throw is to toss a cast-iron skillet 30 feet and knock the head off a dummy without hitting its body. Why do they do it? Perhaps for even suggesting that women and skillets go together. The champion skillet thrower not only receives a prize, but also gets very little lip from the rest of her family during the next twelve months.

East and North Sts., Macksburg, IA 50155

No phone

Hours: The third Sunday in June

Cost: Free

www.orient-macks.k12.ia.us/comunity/skillet/skillet.html

Directions: At the intersection of Rte. G61 (North St.) and Rte. P53 (East St.).

. . . AND IN A RELATED STORY

Lori La Deane Adams threw a two-pound rolling pin 175 feet, 5 inches at the 1979 Iowa State Fair, setting a new world record for the sport.

Missouri Valley
The Sunken Bertrand

On April 1, 1865, the steamboat *Bertrand* sank in the Missouri River carrying (among other things) 5,000 gallons of whiskey, $4,000 in Montana gold, and 35,000 pounds of mercury. No humans went down with the ship, but the *Bertrand*'s cargo was lost . . . until a century later.

The river has long since changed its course, leaving the *Bertrand* buried in a field beneath 30 feet of silt and mud. When the ship was uncovered in 1965, more than 200,000 artifacts were unearthed and cataloged—everything from shoes and toys to kerosene lamps and dinnerware. And if you think life on the prairie was all hardship, take a look at the bottles of fancy French mustard and brandied cherries.

Sad to say, but there's one disturbing kicker: only three of the mercury-filled flasks were ever recovered. The rest are lost nearby, poisoning something.

DeSoto National Wildlife Refuge Visitor's Center, 1434 136th Ln., Missouri Valley, IA 51555

(712) 642-4121

E-mail: r3bertrand@fws.gov

Hours: Daily 9 A.M.–4:30 P.M.

Cost: $3/car

http://refuges.fws.gov/GeneralInterest/SteamBoatBertrand.html

Directions: Seven miles west of Missouri Valley on Rte. 30.

All hail, CORRRRRNNNNN!!!!!!!!

Mount Ayr
Corny Mural

For all corn has done for this great state, you'd think the citizenry would do something in its honor. Dedicate a shrine. Throw it a parade. Build a palace.

In fact, the folks of Sioux City erected just such a corny edifice in 1887. The 18,000-square foot Corn Palace opened to the public on October 3, with a grand stairway of maize and a mosaic U.S. map fashioned from colored kernels. Every inch of the building was covered in seeds, husks, stalks, or cobs. President Grover Cleveland even diverted his train to visit the Corn Palace—it was that remarkable.

Sioux City continued to build more elaborate palaces each fall for the next several years until a deadly flood in the spring of 1892 dampened enthusiasm for a celebration, and planning ceased. That same year the folks of Mitchell, South Dakota, ripped off the idea and ran with it. The Mitchell Corn Palace survives to this day, but the Sioux City Corn Palace? Forget it.

So what's a corn lover to do? Here's an idea: drive on down to the Mount Ayr post office, home of the WPA-era mural *The Corn Parade*. Painted by Orr C. Fisher in 1941, *The Corn Parade* proclaims "Corn Is King." Indeed it is.

Mount Ayr Post Office, 202 W. Madison St., Mount Ayr, IA 50854

(641) 464-2404

Hours: Monday–Friday 6:45 A.M.–5 P.M., Saturday 6:45 A.M.–4 P.M.

Cost: Free

Directions: Just northwest of the town square, at Fillmore St.

Shenandoah
Iowa Walk of Fame

As you probably already know, Iowa has given the world its fair share of celebrities, from Donna Reed to William Frawley, from Wyatt Earp to Johnny Carson. But unlike the folks in Hollywood, Iowa has never had a Walk of Fame.

. . . Until now! When the folks of Shenandoah decided to spruce up their downtown, they turned the town's main drag, Sheridan Avenue, into the Iowa Walk of Fame. Every celebrity discussed in this book, with the possible exception of the wildly popular Cherry Sisters (see page 188) has been immortalized on his or her own tan plaque. Each marker shows the celebrity's hometown on an outline of the state and is embedded in the sidewalk. Sadly, few of Iowa's 100+ stars have ever visited Shenandoah to acknowledge the honor. But that's understandable; many of them are dead.

"Why Shenandoah?" you ask. Why not? The town has contributed a couple stars to the celebrity sky: Don and Phil Everly. The duo got their start here on the KMA radio station. On July 5, 1986, the pair returned to Shenandoah for a Homecoming Concert. A historic marker was erected next to the train depot to commemorate the event. Interestingly enough, no more than fifteen feet away is another plaque marking the spot where Teddy Roosevelt delivered a stump speech eighty years earlier. *That's* why Shenandoah!

Sheridan Ave., Shenandoah, IA 51601

(712) 246-3455

E-mail: chamber@simplyshenandoah.com

Hours: Always visible

Cost: Free

www.simplyshenandoah.com

Directions: Between Railroad St. and Broad St. on Sheridan Ave.

Sidney
Worldly Dirt

Robert Frost once observed, "[Iowa soil] looks good enough to eat without putting it through vegetables." Less tempting, however, is a collection of soil samples at the Fremont County Historical Museum Complex in Sidney. A local woman and her family have collected dirt from about 40 famous locations around the world, from Buckingham Palace to Iwo Jima and the Panama Canal to the White House. Each sample is in a neatly labeled jar, and each one looks more pitiful than the next—when compared to the rich, dark soil of Iowa, that is.

Fremont County Historical Museum Complex, Cass and Indiana Sts., Sidney, IA 51652

(712) 374-3248 or (712) 374-2335 or (712) 385-8229 or (712) 374-2320

E-mail: ebirkby@heartland.net

Hours: June–September, Sunday 1–4 P.M.

Cost: Free

http://bitwind.net/museum.htm

Directions: On Rte. 275 (Main/Indiana St.), one block south of Rte. 2 (Filmore St.), on the east side of the square.

STANTON

Stanton calls itself the Little White City because almost every house and business is painted white. Some residents who dared challenge the tradition have returned home from vacation to find their homes repainted.

Why Stanton's jumpy.

Stanton
World's Largest Coffee Pot and Coffee Cup Water Towers

Long before Starbucks-mania swept the nation, the folks in Stanton decided to build a shrine to coffee. In 1971 they erected a Swedish coffee pot capable of holding 640,000 cups of coffee—that's 40,000 gallons! While that might seem like a bit over the top for a town of 700 residents, don't worry; they filled it with water. Yes, this big-ass brewer is actually the town's water tower.

And *why* did these Swedes choose to decorate their water tower in this manner? One reason: Stanton is the hometown of Virginia Christine, best known to television viewers as Mrs. Olson of Folgers Coffee fame. She also played a nosy bigot in *Guess Who's Coming to Dinner*, but few people remember that role. Christine was born in Stanton in 1920.

In 2000, when the original tower proved inadequate for the town's needs, a second tower was erected. This one was designed to look like a coffee cup, again painted with a Swedish tollware design. The new tower holds 150,000 gallons, or 2.4 million cups.

As you gaze up at the giant coffee pot or coffee cup, perhaps it's a good time to get some perspective on the current state of coffee in America. In 2002, the average American (including children) drank 1.64 cups of coffee per day. With 290 million citizens, that's 476 million cups of joe. In Stanton terms, that's about 743 jumbo coffee pots worth, or 198 colossal coffee cups. *Every day.* And you thought terrorists were making us jumpy.

Coffee Pot, Thorn St. and Grand Ave., Stanton, IA 51573

Coffee Cup, Hilltop and Highland Aves., Stanton, IA 51573

No phone

Hours: Always visible

Cost: Free

www.stantoniowa.com and www.fmtcnet.com/stanton_ia.htm

Directions: Coffee Pot, corner of Thorn St. and Grand Ave., one block east of Halland Ave. and one block north of Frankfort St. on the east side of town; Coffee Cup, corner of Hilltop Ave. and Highland Ave., one block west of Halland Ave. and one block south of the railroad tracks on the south side of town.

TABOR

Abolitionist **John Brown** stored 200 guns in the home of Reverend John Todd (705 Park Street) of Tabor. Brown used the firearms during raids into Kansas in 1856. The home was also a stop on the Underground Railroad.

Chop, chop.
Photo by author, courtesy of Darwin Linn.

Villisca
The Ax Murder House

Folks who attended the Villisca Presbyterian Church's Children's Day Program (109 S. Third Avenue) on Sunday, June 9, 1912, had no idea that their little town would be front page news across the nation the next day. Local businessman Josiah "Joe" Moore was in attendance that night, along with his wife, Sara, and their four children, Herman, Katherine, Boyd, and Paul. At the end of the event, the family retired to their home on Second Street, joined by two of the children's friends, Lena and Ina Stillinger. It was the last time anyone saw them alive.

Sometime after midnight a killer entered the house and systematically murdered all eight victims while they slept. The murderer used the Moores' own ax, which was found at the scene. The killer left no fingerprints and washed up before leaving. Police were unable to name a suspect, but many in town believed State Senator Frank F. Jones was somehow involved.

There was plenty of bad blood between Frank Jones and Joe Moore. Jones had hired Moore to work at his hardware store, and when Moore quit, he took the John Deere franchise with him . . . and opened a new dealership across the street from his old employer. And then there was that unpleasantness about Moore having an affair with the wife of Albert Jones, Frank Jones's oldest son.

Four years after the murders, the Burns Detective Agency dragged in William "Blackie" Mansfield, whose wife, daughter, and in-laws had been chopped up in Blue Island, Illinois, in 1914. Though he was never fingered in his own family's killings, the detectives believed he had been hired by Frank and Albert Jones to kill Joe Moore, and got a little carried away. High on cocaine, the detectives said. A Villisca grand jury didn't buy it, and refused to hand down an indictment. Mansfield sued the agency for wrongful arrest and won a $2,225 cash award. Senator Jones then tried to sue agent James Wilkerson for slander, but a Villisca jury was less sympathetic to the senator's case. He got nothing. Actually, he got even less: he lost his bid for reelection in 1916.

Suspicion then turned to Reverend George Jacklin Kelly, who had given a guest sermon at the Children's Day Program at the Presbyterian Church that fateful night. Though the parishioners didn't know it at the time, Kelly had a rap sheet that included sending notes to young girls asking them to type letters to him while in the nude. He also had several Peeping Tom arrests and a conviction for burning down a barn, on God's orders, he claimed. Kelly had departed Villisca abruptly on a 5:19 A.M. train on June 10 and reportedly spoke with an elderly couple about the murders—*even though the bodies had not yet been found.* Bingo! Authorities then learned Kelly had also sent a bloody shirt out to be laundered a few weeks after the murders. (Why this detail took four years to uncover is unclear.) Confronted with the evidence, Kelly confessed to authorities. He then elaborated on his confession. And then he recanted it. Still, with all this damning circumstantial evidence, his trial ended in a hung jury. The murders remain unsolved to this day.

Unlike so many places that shun or ignore their town's criminal history, most of Villisca embraces the story. The owners of the local history museum purchased the murder house and are restoring it to its 1912 appearance. Tours can be arranged through the Olson-Linn Museum, and are sometimes conducted at night, by lamplight. You'll see the windows covered with clothing and tablecloths, just as they had been covered by the murderer. The owners are negotiating to get a hold of the ax used that night, but it is currently in the possession of another Villisca resident. Sleepovers are also available. To get the full Villisca ax murder experience, be sure to visit the Moore graves at the local cemetery (Fifth Avenue and High Street). The family is lined up in a row with a single, very long tombstone.

508 E. Second St., Villisca, IA 50864

Contact: Olson-Linn Museum, Village Square, 323 E. Fourth St., Villisca, IA 50864

(712) 826-2756 or (641) 322-4202

E-mail: dmlinn@mddc.com

Hours: By appointment, January–April, Saturday–Sunday 1–4 P.M.; May–October, daily 9 A.M.–4 P.M.; Lamplight tours at 8 P.M. by appointment

Cost: Daytime tours $10; Lamplight tours $20

www.villiscaiowa.com or www.villisca.com

Directions: Two blocks east of Fourth Ave. (Rte. H42), one block north of Third St. (Rte. H54).

Winterset
Birthplace of John Wayne

On May 26, 1907, Mary Brown Morrison gave birth to a 13-pound (ouch!) baby boy, Marion Robert Morrison, in a simple Winterset home. Never heard of the kid? When Marion's brother Robert was born, his father, Clyde, changed Marion's middle name to Michael. Young Marion had an Airedale named Duke and adopted the dog's name as his own. Yes, it's a confusing mishmash, which is probably why film director Raoul Walsh, a fan of General Mad Anthony Wayne, gave his new actor Marion Morrison a more butch stage name: John Wayne.

Back in 1907, Marion's father was a pharmacist who worked in a drugstore on the south side of the Winterset town square. The family lived in town until Marion was three, when they moved to nearby Earlham (to 320 Ohio Street). Wayne's Winterset birthplace was restored to its 1907 appearance and opened to the public, filled with Duke-abilia. Everyone wants to see his *True Grit* eye patch (one of 15 he used during his 1969 Best Actor Oscar–winning performance), but they've also got his *Rio Lobo* cowboy hat and plenty of other fake cowboy stuff. If you come to Winterset on July 4, you can also participate in the town's annual John Wayne Festival.

By the way, for all Wayne's macho posturing, it is worth noting that he (1) never worked a cattle drive, (2) never served in the military, (3) hated horses, and (4) was terrified—*terrified*—of snakes. So much for Mr. Tough Guy. . . .

216 S. Second St., Winterset, IA 50273

(515) 462-1044

E-mail: director@johnwaynebirthplace.org

Hours: Daily 10 A.M.–4:30 P.M.

Cost: Adults $2.50, Seniors (55+) $2.25, Kids (12 and under) $1

www.johnwaynebirthplace.org

Directions: One block east of Rte. 169 (John Wayne Dr.), at South Street.

WAUKEE

Mrs. Lana Scott moved from Alaska to Waukee by mailing all of her possessions in 800 packages.

The Bridges of Madison County

Setting aside the question of why Robert James Waller's book *The Bridges of Madison County* captured the reading public's imagination in the early 1990s (see below), there is no denying it single-handedly injected both romance and cold hard cash into the Winterset community. It is the tale of a middle-aged photographer, Robert Kincaid, who meets an immigrant Iowa woman, Francesca Johnson, while shooting the county's six covered bridges for *National Geographic*. With her husband and kids out of town, Francesca falls madly in love with Robert, and he falls for her. Robert photographs the bridges. Francesca makes dinner. They hump on the kitchen table. They hump in the clawfoot tub. And a few days later, both return to their previous lives, forever joined in their hearts, if not in proximity.

Yeah, that's pretty much it.

There were once 19 covered bridges around Winterset, but only seven when the book was published. The best known, the 1883 Roseman Bridge (sometimes referred to as Francesca's Bridge), is reportedly haunted by a man who was hanged by the rafters in 1892 after being framed for theft. His accuser? A father who feared the guy would marry his daughter. Now *that's* romantic!

In 1983 a local man, jilted by his married lover, tried to burn the woman's initials off the McBride Bridge. (He had carved them on it when times were better.) He ended up burning everybody's initials off when the whole structure caught fire. It has never been rebuilt. Then, on September 3, 2002, an arsonist torched Cedar Bridge, the only bridge that was still open to auto traffic. Waller offered a $10,000 reward for information leading to its destroyer. Nobody has ever come forward to claim the money. Meanwhile, plans are underway to rebuild the bridge.

Clint Eastwood came to Winterset in 1994 to film an adaptation of Waller's book. Shot entirely on site, the 1995 movie spawned a whole new set of tourist destinations. Clint (as Robert Kincaid) sits in the Northside Cafe (61 Jefferson Street, (515) 462-1523), fourth seat from the door, and learns more about the town. He stops by a farmhouse to ask for directions and meets Francesca (Meryl Streep). They have a picnic at an old stone bridge (City Park, Ninth and High streets).

Francesca's home in the movie was once an abandoned house west of Cumming. After the movie was released, it became a popular tourist destination. Visitors could slow dance in the kitchen, pose with Harry the Pickup, or sit in the clawfoot tub. On October 6, 2003, like two covered bridges before it, the home was set ablaze by an arsonist. The fire was extinguished before it destroyed the house, but it is no longer open to the public.

One almost wonders if Waller's book wasn't as much a curse as a blessing. Whatever the case, Winterset marches on, hosting a Bridges Festival on the second full weekend each October. For those who still want more, why not get married at the Roseman Bridge? A local wedding planner, Married in Madison County, can arrange the whole show (www.bridgeweddings.com, (515) 462-4435).

Madison County Chamber of Commerce, 73 W. Jefferson St., Winterset, IA 50273

(800) 298-6119 or (515) 462-1185

E-mail: chamber@dwx.com

Hours: Bridges always visible

Cost: Free

www.madisoncounty.com/movie.html

Directions: On the northeast corner of the town square, just west of Rte. 169 (John Wayne Dr.).

WHAT'S ALL THE FUSS ABOUT?

A reader should always be suspicious when, on page 8, a novel's main character rolls off his latest sexual conquest, and that woman proclaims, "You're the best, Robert, no competition, not even close." A reader should be particularly suspicious if that story of someone named Robert Kincaid, a fifty something writer/photographer with long, gray hair, has been penned by Robert Waller, a fifty something writer/photographer with long, gray hair. Does Waller's Kinkaid have any faults . . . except that he loves too hard, cares too much, lives too fully, and romances too passionately?

Gimme a break. Robert James Waller has bragged that he wrote *The Bridges of Madison County* in 14 days. I would have guessed five, tops. How this run-of-the-mill romance novel became a "classic" is a mystery. Still, the book isn't completely without its high points. The most honest writing comes when Robert explains to Francesca the downside of working for *National Geographic*: "That's the problem in earning a living through an art form. You're always dealing with markets, and markets—mass markets—are designed to suit average tastes."

I'm with you there, Rob!

Quite an honor.
Photo by author, courtesy of the Madison County Historical Complex.

Historic Crapper

It should be said up front that the Madison County Historical Complex is one of the best of its kind in Iowa. It's comprised of a dozen historic buildings, including the Bevington-Kaser House, a log school, and a train depot. All interesting, each and every one. But whatever you do, don't leave without seeing the complex's Historic Crapper.

Of course, they don't call it the Historic Crapper. It's the C. D. and Eliya Heath Bevington Privvy. Still, it *is* listed on the National Register of Historic Places, and it *is* an outhouse—ergo, the Historic Crapper. This three-hole stone facility, built in 1856, serviced the Bevington-Kaser House and was both heated and wallpapered in its day. As long as you have to use a pit toilet, you might as well sit in style!

Madison County Historical Complex, 815 S. Second Ave., Winterset, IA 50273

(515) 462-2134

E-mail: mchistory@i-rule.net

Hours: May–October, Monday–Saturday 11 A.M.–4 P.M., Sunday 1–5 P.M.

Cost: Adults $3, Kids (12 and under) Free

Directions: Two blocks south of Summit St. (Rte. P71), two blocks west of John Wayne
Dr. (Rte. 169).

Who'd a thunk?

Iowa's Only Tunnel

Iowa gets a bad rap as a flat state; it's actually covered in beautiful rolling
hills. Yet few of those hills are high enough and steep enough to require
a tunnel for drivers to pass through. However, Iowa does have one tunnel, and it's located in Pammel State Park.

Back in 1858, William Harmon and his three sons dug a tunnel through the black shale of Devil's Backbone along Badger Creek. The goal was to allow water to pass though in order to power their saw mill (which they later converted to a grist mill). The mill closed in 1904 and the tunnel sat idle. In 1925 it was converted to a highway tunnel. You can still drive through it today, though there is a sign warning motorists to avoid the route during high water—remember the tunnel's original use.

Harmon Tunnel, Pammel State Park, Rte. 322, Winterset, IA 50273

(515) 462-3536

Hours: Always visible

Cost: Free

www.madisoncountyparks.org/parks/pammel.htm

Directions: Head west out of town on Rte. 92, then south on Rte. 322 to the park.

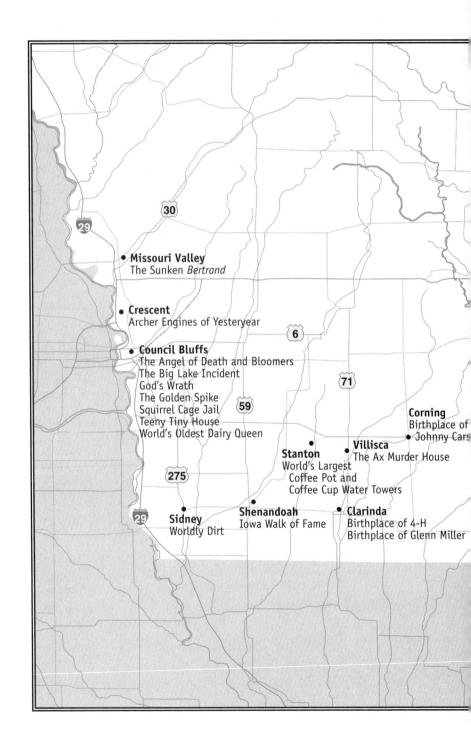

Missouri Valley
The Sunken *Bertrand*

Crescent
Archer Engines of Yesteryear

Council Bluffs
The Angel of Death and Bloomers
The Big Lake Incident
God's Wrath
The Golden Spike
Squirrel Cage Jail
Teeny Tiny House
World's Oldest Dairy Queen

Corning
Birthplace of
Johnny Carson

Stanton
World's Largest
Coffee Pot and
Coffee Cup Water Towers

Villisca
The Ax Murder House

Sidney
Worldly Dirt

Shenandoah
Iowa Walk of Fame

Clarinda
Birthplace of 4-H
Birthplace of Glenn Miller

Winterset
Birthplace of
John Wayne
*The Bridges of
Madison County* ● **East Peru**
Historic Crapper   Birthplace of the
Iowa's Only Tunnel Delicious Apple

●
Macksburg
National Skillet Throw

Creston
Frank Phillips Tourism
Information Center

Mount Ayr
● Corny Mural

Missouri

4

THE SOUTHEAST

ou can't get any lower in Iowa than in the southeast corner of the state. I'm not talking culturally, or genetically, I'm talking *literally*: Keokuk is a mere 480 feet above sea level, which is 1,190 feet lower than the state's highest peak. OK, make that the state's highest bump. In just four chapters you've sunk pretty low—down, down, down to the very dregs of the Hawkeye State, the Mississippi bottomlands, where every sort of belly-dragging, mud-sucking life form seems to have found a home under a rock.

Naaaahh—I'm just kidding. Quite to the contrary, the southeast region has attracted more than a few lofty attractions, such as the National Balloon Museum in Indianola, the yogic flyers in Vedic City, the Lovers Leap Bridge in Columbus Junction, and the otherworldly future birthplace of Captain James T. Kirk in Riverside. If you're more down-to-earth, check out Varner's Caboose in Montpelier, the Mule Cemetery in Oskaloosa, or Trainland U.S.A. in Colfax. Still, if you're determined to slither along the ground, may I suggest Snake Alley in Burlington?

Check your brakes before you visit.

Burlington
Snake Alley

Back in the early 1890s, Burlington was essentially two towns: the riverfront business district and the hilltop residential district, known as Heritage Hill. To connect the two, Charles Starker, William Steyh, and George Kriechbaum came up with a plan: build a shortcut connecting Washington Street (downtown) with Columbia Street (uptown). Snake Alley opened in 1894. Though it is only 275 feet long, it rises 58.3 feet through five half-turns and two quarter-turns. The paving bricks were placed with an angular layout to afford horses a better footing; it didn't always work, as there were many reports of runaway wagons.

Ripley's Believe It or Not! claims that Snake Alley is the Crookedest Street in the World, which may or may not be true—what about Wall Street?—but it certainly is the Crookedest Street in Iowa. The alley is still open to traffic, though today it is a one-way street, going down. On Memorial Day each year the traffic is reversed, but for bikes only. The 80-mile Snake Alley Criterium starts at the bottom of the hill and weeds out the wusses in the first 100 yards of the race.

N. Sixth St., Burlington, IA 52601

(800) 82-RIVER or (319) 752-6365

E-mail: whogan@growburlington.com

Hours: Always there

Cost: Free

www.visit.burlington.ia.us/history.html#snake

Directions: South two blocks on Central St. from Rte. 34, left (east) on Columbia St. for three blocks, then right onto Snake Alley, down to Washington St.

BETTENDORF
A fat maid is said to haunt Bettendorf's Central Avenue. A helpful spirit, she enters homes and washes the owners' clothes.

BURLINGTON
William "Fred Mertz" Frawley was born in Burlington on February 26, 1887.

An octagon-shaped UFO was spotted over Burlington on January 26, 1996. Then, on August 12 of the same year, a cigar-shaped craft "swallowed" an ultralight plane and its pilot over a city park.

They would have needed a shoehorn.

Carlisle
The McCaughey Septuplets

When the news first leaked out in early November 1997, it was hard to believe: an Iowa woman was pregnant with *seven* children. Even more amazing was that Bobbi and Kenny McCaughey kept it secret for as long as they did, since many of the folks in their hometown of Carlisle already knew. Bobbi had been taking the fertility drug Metrodin, and boy did it work! Because of their religious beliefs, the McCaugheys opted not to have a "selective reduction" of the fetuses, choosing instead to carry all of them for as long as was medically possible. Thirty weeks into the pregnancy, on November 19, 1997, Bobbi gave birth to Alexis,

Brandon, Joel, Kelsey, Kenneth, Natalie, and Nathan at the Iowa Methodist Medical Center in Des Moines (1200 Pleasant Street, (515) 241-6212), assisted by staff from Blank Children's Hospital (1212 Pleasant Street, (515) 241-5437), which is attached to Iowa Methodist. Six minutes after the cesarean started, Bobbi was 50 pounds lighter and well on her way to racking up a $1 million+ hospital bill. The operation alone required 66 doctors, nurses, and medical technicians, to say nothing of the premature birth care the septuplets needed during their first months. Thank God for health insurance . . . and the McCaugheys most certainly did.

Back in Carlisle, the McCaugheys owned a small three-bedroom home, hardly big enough for a family of ten. (They already had one daughter, Mikayla.) The media attention, however, brought a flood of donations, including a new five-bedroom home, a lifetime supply of Pampers and Gerber baby food, a year's supply of groceries from HyVee Foods, a $10,000 check from Julia Roberts, a 15-passenger van from Kenny's employer, Wright Chevrolet (95 Route 5, (515) 989-0811), and college scholarships for the whole gang. Best of all, their Missionary Baptist Church (615 Route 5, (515) 989-3801) organized a McCaughey Committee to provide nearly round-the-clock childcare volunteers. That's right, Bobbi and Kenny were able to get eight hours of sleep every night, two hours of alone time each morning, and every Friday night out. How many new parents get that kind of freedom?

The family's on its own now and doing quite well, with only minor medical challenges. Bobbi later became a spokesperson for Simplicity, while Kenny did commercials for Black & Decker.

McCaughey's Former Home, 615 First St., Carlisle, IA 50047
Private phone
Hours: Always visible
Cost: Free
Directions: Seven blocks north of Rte. 5 on First St.

Colfax
Trainland U.S.A.
After being visited by aliens in the movie *Close Encounters of the Third Kind*, the character played by Richard Dreyfus becomes obsessed with

building a scale model of Devils Tower in Wyoming. Leland "Red" Atwood of Colfax had a similar obsession, though there is no indication that little green men had anything to do with it. He started collecting O-gauge Lionel trains in 1964, and his hobby sort of got out of hand. In 1976 Atwood decided he wanted to build the world's largest train layout, so he tore down his home and rebuilt a new structure on the site, specially designed to accommodate his O-gauge vision.

Five years later it was done: Trainland U.S.A.! The layout covers 2,600 square feet, with 4,000 feet of track rolling over 35,000 hand-cut railroad ties. Between 20 and 25 trains are in service at any one time. Trainland U.S.A. has more than 200 buildings and structures, including a White House, a Statue of Liberty, a working Kentucky coal mine, and a drive-in movie theater with cartoons projected on the screen. Atwood incorporated dozen of unique features, such as a moonshine still, ice skaters that glide across a frozen pond, a man being hanged at Boot Hill, Mount Rushmore, San Francisco cable cars, and, yes, Devils Tower. Hmmmmm. . . .

3135 Rte. 117N, Colfax, IA 50054

(515) 674-3813

E-mail: judy@trainland-usa.com

Hours: June–August, daily 10 A.M.–6 P.M.

Cost: Adults $4.50, Seniors (55+) $4, Kids (2–12) $2

www.trainlandusa.com

Directions: Two miles north of I-80 on Rte. 117.

DAVENPORT

The world's first appendicitis operation was performed on Mary Gartside by Dr. William Grant of Davenport on January 4, 1883.

The Mercy Hospital in Davenport burned on January 7, 1950, after a smoker set a wing afire. Forty mental patients died.

Hold on. Really.

Columbus Junction
Lovers Leap Bridge

Lovers in Columbus Junction must be a wild bunch, because the foot-bridge named after them swings more than Hugh Hefner's Playboy Mansion. The original Lovers Leap Bridge was constructed in 1886 of barrel staves and wire, but stilts were soon added because the bridge rocked too much. In 1902 the bridge was condemned due to safety concerns, but a new, longer bridge was erected two years later. The 160-foot-long swinging bridge survived until 1920 when it snapped, dropping two unsuspecting pedestrians into the chasm below. (They survived.)

Apparently nobody learned their lesson, for an even longer swing bridge was built in 1922, this one connecting the full 262 feet between Third and Fourth streets. The cables and planking were replaced in 1954, but other than that, it's pretty much the same structure today.

If you're planning on crossing Lovers Leap Bridge, be forewarned that it really does swing. A *lot*. Back and forth, side to side, particularly when more than one person is walking on it at the same time. Local legend says that an Indian maiden threw herself into this crevasse after hearing that her lover had perished in a battle, hence the name. Today you don't have to jump—the bridge will probably toss you overboard.

Columbus Junction Swinging Bridge, Third St., Columbus Junction, IA 52738

No phone

Hours: Always visible

Cost: Free

www.cjiowa.com

Directions: South of Oak St. (Rte. 92) on Third St.; the bridge connects Third and Fourth Sts.

Davenport
The Brady Street Banshee

Alfred Schacht and his family weren't born under a dark cloud; they moved under it. In 1918 the Schachts purchased a Victorian home on Brady Street, and very soon things started going terribly, terribly wrong. First, the Schachts' seven-year-old son fell from an attic window and was impaled on a fencepost out front; locals whispered he was pushed by a mysterious hobo. Next, the family's teenage daughter drowned in an unexplained bathtub mishap. A distraught Mrs. Schacht hung herself in the basement. Alone and depressed, Alfred was soon swinging from the rafters, too, though he killed himself in the kitchen. All four deaths occurred within a year of the family moving in.

Needless to say, realtors had a hard time moving the empty and presumably cursed home. The price continued to drop until a Mafia henchman spotted what he thought was a bargain. A few of his "lady friends" moved in and set up a brothel that became a popular hideout for denizens of the Chicago underworld. (Al Capone even spent some time there.) It became less popular—to the point of emptiness—when ghosts began to appear. The worst spirit was a wailing hag dubbed the Brady Street Banshee.

The building later was used as a boarding house for college students. Cold drafts . . . moans and screams . . . covers ripped from the beds in the middle of the night. It didn't sit well with the residents, and soon there were no boarders. The house fell into disrepair and was eventually torn down, replaced with a parking lot.

So where did the spirits go? The most repeated rumor in Davenport is that the ghosts moved into new homes along Brady Street. Which lucky building ended up with the Brady Street Banshee? Nobody's talking. Property values, you understand. . . .

Brady Street, Davenport, IA 52803

No phone

Hours: Always visible

Cost: Free

Directions: Two blocks east of Rte. 61 (Harrison St.).

The Davenport Stone

It's a fake . . . or so some say. What is it, and who are *they*? The Davenport Stone and the know-it-alls at the Putnam Museum.

Before getting into the controversy surrounding the stone, it is important to understand where it all started. In January 1877, Reverend Jacob Gass unearthed a pair of inscribed stones while digging through a Native American burial mound near town. The first slab appeared to be a calendar stone, while the other, the Davenport Stone, showed three Old World alphabets (Egyptian, Punic-Iberian, and Libyan-Moroccan), a hunting scene, and a depiction of a cremation ceremony.

In those days digs weren't conducted so much by trained archaeologists with dust brushes and tweezers as by local enthusiasts with picks and shovels. Gass was no exception; he was a member of the Davenport Academy of Natural Sciences, which was actually a gentlemen's exploration club. Gass presented the stones to the rest of the members who hailed the discovery and shipped the stones off to the Smithsonian for analysis.

The Smithsonian praised the find, then claimed it could be a hoax, then returned to its original verdict. Enter John Wesley Powell, the Smithsonian's new Director of Ethnology. This famed Grand Canyon explorer believed all claims of pre-Columbian explorers in North America to be hogwash, and he wasn't about to let the Smithsonian endorse such foolish theories. Powell had also received a letter from a certain Mr. Tiffany of the Davenport Academy claiming that two other artifacts Gass had discovered, an effigy pipe and a limestone tablet, were fakes he (Tiffany) had created and used to embarrass Mr. Fancypants Mound-Digger. Powell used this letter to denounce Gass out of hand, and stories were circulated that the Davenport Stone was really just a hunk of slate pulled off the side of a local whorehouse, scratched up with fake etchings, and buried in the mound for Gass to find.

Tiffany and his coconspirator, Dr. Lindley, were immediately and unanimously voted out of the Davenport Academy. The stone faded from view, and the Academy turned over its collection to the newly founded Putnam Museum. Though no definitive evidence was ever presented to back up the claims of the stone's detractors, the current Putnam Museum staff are holding strong to the hoax theory. The Davenport Stone is still in the museum's possession, but it is not on display . . . *until* the people demand the vaults be opened!

Putnam Museum of History and Natural Science, 1717 W. Twelfth St., Davenport, 52804

(319) 324-1933

Hours: Monday–Friday 9 A.M.–5 P.M., Saturday 10 A.M.–5 P.M., Sunday 11 A.M.–5 P.M.

Cost: Adults $6, Seniors (60+) $5, Kids (3–12) $4

www.putnam.org

Directions: Thirteen blocks north of Rte. 61 (River Rd.) on Division St., to Twelfth St.

DAVENPORT

Ashley Wilkes was held in Davenport's Confederate prison in *Gone with the Wind*.

All alone.

Mother Goose in a Zoo

Just inside the entrance to the petting zoo at Fejervary Park is a goose-shaped structure. She wears a floppy blue hat and a pair of wire spectacles, and has a large doorway where her chest should be. What's she doing here?

This odd bird was once the entrance to Mother Goose Land, a nursery rhyme–themed kiddie park that stood on this site. Children could ride burros or explore the park's many downsized fairy-tale buildings. All of it is gone today. All, that is, except Mother Goose. The petting zoo is nice enough, but it is sad to contemplate what once was, and will likely never be again.

Fejervary Park Children's Zoo, 1800 W. Twelfth St., Davenport, IA 52804
(563) 326-7812

Hours: Always visible; Petting Zoo, May and September–October, Saturday 10 A.M.–5 P.M., Sunday Noon–5 P.M.; June–August, Tuesday–Saturday, 10 A.M.–5 P.M., Sunday Noon–5 P.M.

Cost: Free, Petting Zoo, Adults $2.50, Seniors (62+) $2, Kids (5–17) $2

www.cityofdavenportiowa.com/leisure/parks/fej.htm

Directions: Thirteen blocks north of Rte. 61 (River Rd.) on Division St., to Twelfth St.

Palmer College

When Daniel David "D.D." Palmer first embarked on a career in medicine, he tried curing his patients through the use of magnets. This method wasn't nearly as successful as an alternative therapy he discovered in 1895: chiropractics. Palmer's half-deaf janitor had mentioned that he had lost his hearing on the same day he twisted his neck, and Palmer theorized that the two were related—all he had to do was realign the man's vertebrae! After a few cracks, the overly trustful man's hearing returned.

Palmer chucked the magnets and in 1897 opened a chiropractic school at Second and Brady streets in Davenport. A friend suggested he use the word *chiropractics*—a combination of *cheir* and *praktikos*, Greek for "hand" and "done"—to describe the new procedures. Palmer's son, Bartlett Joshua, or B.J., followed in his father's footsteps. With the help of his wife, Mabel Heath, B.J. expanded the school, opening a new campus at its present location in 1906. To get the word out, the Palmers launched radio station WOC in the late 1920s. Ronald Reagan worked for WOC for a short time in 1932—his first broadcasting job out of college—before moving on to a Des Moines station.

Palmer College still trains chiropractors. Three enormous, spooky busts of D.D., B.J., and Mabel have been installed in a courtyard adjoining Lyceum Hall. According to reports, the Palmers had amassed the world's largest collection of spinal columns in the course of their studies. Some of the mounted spines are still on display at Lyceum Hall.

Palmer College, 1000 Brady Street, Davenport, IA 52803

(800) 722-3648 or (563) 884-5656

E-mail: pcadmit@palmer.edu

Hours: Always visible

Cost: Free

www.palmer.edu

Directions: On Rte. 61 (Brady St.) between Eighth and Eleventh Sts.

DAVENPORT

The August 21, 1814, Battle of Credit Island in Davenport, between U.S. troops and Sioux and Winnebago warriors backed by the British, was the only international conflict ever fought on Iowa soil.

Des Moines
The Butter Cow Lady

Norma "Duffy" Lyon is an Iowa institution. For 40 years she sculpted full-size cows for the Iowa State Fair . . . out of butter. They continue to be the fair's most popular attraction.

As a child, Lyon wanted to be a veterinarian, but when she attended Iowa State that major was not open to women. Instead, she studied animal science. In the winter of 1948 she carved a snow sculpture of a horse pulling a sleigh in front of her Alpha Delta Pi sorority. It caught the attention of Christian Petersen, an art instructor, who invited her to attend his sculpture classes. The rest is butter-carving history.

The Iowa State Fair had been displaying butter cows since 1911, the first crafted by J.E. Wallace, but Duffy Lyon was the first woman to get the job. The fair commissioned Lyon to create her first butter cow, a Jersey, in 1960, and she did it every subsequent year until 2000. It takes about 500 to 600 pounds of butter, a wooden armature, and a very large cooler set at 42°F to build a butter cow. The butter, frozen between fairs, can be used for up to five years before it turns rancid.

For years, Lyon rotated among the six major dairy breeds: Ayrshire, Brown Swiss, Holstein, Jersey, Guernsey, and Milking Shorthorn. As she became more skilled, she veered from the traditional designs. On three occasions she crafted cows that produced milk when their teats were pulled. She also made life-sized re-creations of Elvis, Hansel and Gretel outside a gingerbread house, Garth Brooks, a bear riding a unicycle, Dwight and Mamie Eisenhower, and Grant Wood's *American Gothic*. In 1999 she re-created da Vinci's *The Last Supper*.

Lyons has retired, but the Iowa State Fair continues the butter cow tradition and likely will for years to come.

Iowa State Fair, University Ave. and 30th Ave., PO Box 57130, Des Moines, IA 50317

(800) 545-FAIR or (515) 262-3111

E-mail: info@iowastatefair.org

Hours: August, 8 A.M.–1 A.M.

Cost: Adults $8, Kids (6–11) $4

www.iowastatefair.org

Directions: Southeast of the intersection of Rte. 163 (University Ave.) and Rte. 46 (30th Ave.).

Sure, the Iowa State Fair is fun, but it used to be a lot more so. The first fair was held in Fairfield on October 25–27, 1854. Gate receipts totaled $1,000, of which $50 were in counterfeit bills.

For almost forty years, between 1896 to 1932, the fair staged Locomotive Thrill Wrecks. Two train engines were sent careening down the same pair of tracks from opposite directions, timed so that they slammed head-on into one another in front of the grandstands.

But that's not all. The Iowa State Fair also saw the world's first baby contest in 1911. The original idea, called "The Iowa Idea," was to judge the tots as one might judge cattle or pigs. The contest was endorsed by the American Medical Association, but was discontinued in the 1950s when eugenics fell out of favor.

Eddyville
A Headless Treasure

Three prospectors were on their way home from the Black Hills in 1878 when they began fighting over who cheated whom in a poker game. William Gunton lost the debate, and his head, which his two assailants tossed into their campfire.

The next morning, after they sobered up, the killers buried the rest of Gunton's body nearby. They also buried three pots filled with gold, forming a rough triangle around the headless prospector's unmarked grave. Years later the Eddyville postmaster received a deathbed confession from a man named Le Barge, asking that Gunton be exhumed and properly laid to rest. Unfortunately, Le Barge was a little hazy on where the body could be found.

The local folk really didn't give a damn about finding the body, except that it pointed the way to a treasure in gold. Many holes were dug around town, all with similar results: nothing. But when a charred skull turned up when the county grated the old north wagon trail in 1920, a new gold rush was on. If anyone recovered the gold, he or she never told anyone. Most believe the pots are still buried somewhere among the trees north of the town cemetery.

Berdan St., Eddyville, IA 52553

No phone

Hours: Dawn–Dusk

Cost: Free

Directions: Two blocks east of Rte. 63 (Eighth St.) on Rte. G77 (Berdan St.).

DAVENPORT

Jazz cornetist **Leon "Bix" Beiderbecke** lived at 1934 Grand Avenue in Davenport, before dying at age 28 on August 7, 1931. He is buried at Oakdale Memorial Gardens (2501 Eastern Avenue, (563) 324-5121). Davenport hosts the Bix Beiderbecke Memorial Jazz Festival in late July each year.

DES MOINES

Actress **Sada Thompson** was born in Des Moines in September 27, 1929.

The statue of **Abraham Lincoln** and his son Tad outside the Iowa State Capitol (Ninth Street and Grand Avenue) in Des Moines is the only known statue of a U.S. president in a family setting.

Ronald Reagan worked for the WHO radio station in Des Moines from 1933 to 1937. He lived at 330 Center Street and 400 Center Street during his years in the capital. Both homes are now gone.

Actress **Cloris Leachman** was born in Des Moines on April 30, 1926. During her career she was a runner-up for Miss America 1946, won an Oscar for *The Last Picture Show*, and took home four Emmys playing Phyllis Lindstrom on *The Mary Tyler Moore Show*.

Des Moines was originally named Fort Raccoon.

Pitchfork not included.

Eldon
American Gothic House

In 1930 Grant Wood entered a painting in a competition sponsored by the Art Institute of Chicago. It was the portrait of a farmer and his daughter standing in front of a simple home. Wood asked his dentist, Dr. Byron McKeeby, to pose as the farmer, and his sister Nan Wood Graham to be the daughter. For an extra rural touch, Wood posed McKeeby with a pitchfork in his hand. Wood lengthened his sister's head to make her less recognizable, but when she saw herself as a droopy-faced sourpuss, she was less than pleased.

For the painting's backdrop, Wood used a sketch of a home he had made earlier that year while on a road trip through Eldon. The building's unique gothic upper window inspired the painting's title. As he would later learn, the 1881 structure was first used as a brothel.

The Art Institute awarded Wood $300 for the work, titled *American*

Gothic. Per the rules of the competition, the museum kept the prizewinner. What a bargain it turned out to be! Today, *American Gothic* is perhaps the nation's best-known work of art. It is also one of the most parodied. In 1977, *Hustler* published its own rendering, this one more in keeping with the Gothic House's original function: the daughter had hiked up her dress to reveal her ample breasts. Nan Wood Graham was not amused and sued the magazine. The case was later dismissed. Graham's collection of parodies she approved of can be found at the Figge Art Museum (1737 W. Twelfth Street, (563) 326-7804, www.art-dma.org), side by side with the only self-portrait Wood ever painted.

Today the Gothic House is owned by the State Historical Society of Iowa, but it is not open to the public. You can, however, bring your own pitchfork and pose out front. If you come to Eldon in the summer, you might have to stand in line; the town celebrates Gothic Days on the second Saturday each June.

301 American Gothic St., Eldon, IA 52554

(641) 652-3406

E-mail: gothicman@lisco.com

Hours: Daylight hours; view from street

Cost: Free

www.iowahistory.org/sites/gothic_house/gothic_house.html or

  www.grantwoodstudio.org

Directions: Head north on Eldon St. from Elm St. (Rte. 16), turn right on Castor St., then left on Finney St.; follow the signs.

DES MOINES
Amelia Earhart lived at four different Des Moines homes during six years of her childhood, from 1908 to 1914. Two of these houses still stand, at 1443 Eighth Street and 1530 Eighth Street.

Bite this.

Fruitland
World's Largest Watermelon Slice

As local farmers will tell you, there's no better place in the world to raise melons than the Mississippi River floodplains around Muscatine. In fact, the town calls itself Melon City. And if you need any proof of this agricultural achievement, head west out of town on Route 61 to the wide spot in the road known as Fruitland; there you'll find the World's Largest Watermelon Slice. Sorry to say, the wedge was not cut from an actual melon, but built using particle board. Had the watermelon been real, it would have measured 12 feet in diameter.

Hoopes Melon Shed, 4701 Grandview Ave., Fruitland, IA 52749

(563) 263-7302

Hours: Always visible

Cost: Free

Directions: Southwest of the Rte. 61 Bypass with Rte. 61 on Rte. 61 (Grandview Ave.).

Indianola
National Balloon Museum
The Balloon Federation of America opened this unique museum in 1987 as a way of cleaning out its attic. For years, aficionados had been sending their log books, baskets, and other paraphernalia to the organization, so the BFA built a public repository on the north side of Indianola to house it all. It's hard to miss—it looks like two upside-down balloons.

This museum traces the entire history of ballooning in the United States, from the late 1700s on. Gas balloons, uniforms, lapel pins, gondolas, inflator fans, and other artifacts are all on display. The curators also aim to educate visitors about the historical and cultural significance of ballooning: its contribution to flight, its use in warfare, and its present-day popularity as a competitive sport. They've also got a charred piece of the *Hindenburg* as a reminder of one not-so-successful milestone in lighter-than-air history. Be sure to check out the photo exhibit of novelty balloons—inflatable craft in the shapes of Jesus, the Energizer Bunny, a champagne bottle, a Burger King Whopper, a giant ear of corn, and more.

Every August the National Balloon Classic is held in Indianola on the grounds of Simpson College. The four main events are the Convergent Navigational Task, Predetermined Spot Landing, Elbow Task, and Hare and Hounds. If you know anything about ballooning, you know what these are; if you don't know, you should probably stop by the museum first.

1601 N. Jefferson, PO Box 149, Indianola, IA 50125

(515) 961-3714

Hours: February–December, Monday–Friday 9 A.M.–4 P.M., Saturday 10 A.M.–4 P.M., Sunday 1–4 P.M.

Cost: Free

www.nationalballoonmuseum.com

Directions: On Rte. 65/69 (Jefferson) at the north end of town.

DES MOINES
Every winter Des Moines hosts the Skywalk Open, a miniature golf tournament through its downtown skyways.

Do you dare . . . tramp!

Iowa City
Death to Non-Virgins!

Let me say up front, I have nothing against non-virgins. Some of my best friends are non-virgins. Actually, *most* of my friends are non-virgins . . . but that's their business.

The Black Angel of Iowa City feels otherwise. Legend has it that anyone who touches the winged Feldevert Monument in Oakland Cemetery will drop dead, unless he or she is a virgin. Others claim all you need do to incur her wrath is kiss in front of her during a full moon; sluts will be dead within six months. Another legend claims the angel grows blacker each Halloween to mark the impure souls she has claimed in the previous year.

The monument, placed here in 1912 by Teresa Feldevert, was dubbed the Black Angel after its bronze casting oxidized. Stories circulated that it had been cursed by a gypsy woman to remind Feldevert of her marital infidelity. The inscription on the base is written in an old Bohemian dialect, which only adds to the story.

Oakland Cemetery, 1000 Brown St., Iowa City, IA 52245

(319) 356-5105

Hours: Daily 7:30 A.M.–9 P.M.

Cost: Free

www.icgov.org/documents/oaklandhistory.pdf

Directions: One block east of Governor St. on Brown St., on the north side of town.

Knoxville
National Sprint Car Hall of Fame and Museum

Sprint car enthusiasts don't have to be told that Knoxville's the place to go any more than Muslim pilgrims need to be told that they should visit Mecca. They know. For the rest of you, here's the lowdown. Sprint car racing has been around almost as long as there's been auto racing. Sprint cars are open-wheeled racers, and they are fast, noisy, and covered in mud—the way auto racing was meant to be enjoyed.

The Knoxville Raceway has long been the epicenter of sprint car racing, so it was the most logical location to build the sport's Hall of Fame. The three-story museum opened adjacent to Turn 2 in 1991. It contains dozens of historic sprint cars, big cars, and midgets, as well as hundreds of trophies, uniforms, helmets, tires, engines, photographs, and other mud-caked junk.

If you're looking for something a bit more lively, every Saturday night in Knoxville you can catch real races in this, the Sprint Car Capital of the World. Visit in August and you can catch the National Championships . . . and have your eardrums blown out in the process.

Knoxville Raceway, 1 Sprint Capital Pl., Knoxville, IA 50138

(800) 874-4488 or (641) 842-6176

E-mail: sprintcarhof@sprintcarhof.com

Hours: October–March, Monday–Friday 10 A.M.–6 P.M., Saturday–Sunday Noon–5 P.M.; April–September, Monday–Friday 10 A.M.–6 P.M., Saturday 10 A.M.–5 P.M., Sunday Noon–5 P.M.

Cost: Adults $3, Seniors $2, Kids $2

www.sprintcarhof.com

Directions: At the county fairgrounds off Route 14. (Lincoln St.), opposite Larson St., at the north end of town.

King of Clocks.
Photo by author, courtesy of John McLain.

Lockridge
Johnny Clock Museum

Most people feel the need to document their life story. Some keep diaries while others build photo albums. Not John McLain. Born with dyslexia, he found writing frustrating, and he wasn't a photographer, but he discovered he could carve. McLain combined his talent with his love of clocks, and thirty years and fifty clocks later, the Johnny Clock Museum was born.

McLain's story starts with the Sea Captain Clock; a young boy—Johnny—lies in the grass and dreams of sailing the seven seas. It's followed by the Country Home Clock, a vision of his grandparents' farm in southeast Iowa with a display cabinet showing off his grandmother's wedding dress. Yes, this clock is big, floor-to-ceiling big. McLain has hundreds of family heirlooms built into all his creations. There's even an empty repository for storing his and his wife's ashes in the Memories Clock . . . whenever that time comes.

Not every clock in the museum is tied to an event in McLain's life. Some reflect his interest in state history (the Terrace Hill Clock), cartoons (the Disney Clock), country music (the Grand Ole Opry Clock), and folklore (the Paul Bunyan Clock). He's also carved or built every item in the adjoining Indian Room, a roped-off salute to Native American culture in rec-room form.

711 W. Main St., Lockridge, IA 52635

(319) 696-3711

Hours: May–August, Monday–Friday 9 A.M.–5 P.M., or by appointment

Cost: Adults $3

Directions: Two blocks west of Center St. on Rte. W40 (Main St.).

Montpelier
Varner's Caboose

Anyone traveling through Iowa knows that every other town has an old Rock Island caboose sitting in its city park. In Montpelier, however, the caboose you'll see is privately owned and open for business—as a one-room bed & breakfast. The Varners restored the caboose in 1988, adding a TV, microwave, fridge, toilet, shower, central air, and bed space for four. Your breakfast is prepared in advance and will be waiting in the fridge whenever you wake up.

3911 Highway 22E, PO Box 10, Montpelier, IA 52759

(563) 381-3652

Hours: May–November, by reservation

Cost: Two guests, $65; Additional guests $5 each

www.bbonline.com/ia/caboose/

Directions: At the east end of town along Rte. 22, at Dodge St.

Muscatine
Pearl Button Museum

You've probably figured out that pearl buttons aren't really made from pearls, but have you asked yourself where they might come from instead? For many years, the answer would have been Muscatine, Pearl Button Capital of the World.

In 1897 a local man, John Boepple, went swimming in the Mississippi River and cut his foot on a clamshell. Rather than curse his misfortune, he realized he'd tripped over something quite valuable: a seemingly endless supply of raw button material. By 1905, a third of the world's buttons were being manufactured in this town. Half the city's population was employed in one of 40+ factories.

Sadly, the button boom didn't last forever, killed off by the zipper, the Buttonworker Strike of 1911, the Great Depression, and, much later, Velcro. You can learn the whole story at this town's newly renovated Pearl Button Museum. The museum traces the progress from clam to button through the machines used to collect, process, cut, drill, and dye the raw material pulled from the river.

117 W. Second St., Muscatine, IA 52761

(563) 263-1052

E-mail: kurtz@machlink.com

Hours: Tuesday–Saturdays Noon–4 P.M.

Cost: Free

www.pearlbuttoncapital.com

Directions: One block north of Rte. 61 (Mississippi Dr.), between Iowa Ave. and
  Chestnut St.

Phantasuite Hotel

Let's say . . . and we're talking hypothetically . . . you've always wanted to make love in outer space, but don't have the technical skills NASA is looking for. Are you just out of luck? Not if you come to Muscatine. From the outside this Econolodge looks like any other chain hotel, but inside, your fantasy awaits!

Excuse me—*phan*tasy. Though it is no longer associated with the popular Fantasuite franchise, the Econolodge Canterbury Hotel still has all the rooms you need to fulfill your wildest dream. Do you want your mummy? Relax on a sarcophagus-shaped waterbed in the Pharaoh's Chamber. Need an excuse to cuddle up? Crank up the AC and climb under the faux polar-bear-skin comforter in the Northern Lights igloo. Do you deserve to be treated like a princess? Slip into the glass-slipper-shaped whirlpool in the Cinderella suite. And if you're looking to blast off, check out the Space Odyssey; the suite has a Gemini Space Capsule bed and a moon crater hot tub. Sorry, but gravity is included in the package.

In all, the Phantasuite has sixteen themed suites. In addition to those listed above, they've got Cupid's Corner, Sir Lancelot, Roman Villa, Jungle Safari, Arabian Nights, Caesar's Court, Geisha Garden, Queen Anne, Riverboat Gambler, Grecian Getaway, Sherwood Forest, and Henry VIII (no beheadings allowed!). Champagne, chocolates, roses, and silk boxers are available through the front desk.

Econolodge Muscatine Canterbury Hotel, 2402 Park Ave., Muscatine, IA 52761
(800) 234-STAY or (319) 264-3337
Hours: Always open; tours Saturday and Sunday 3 P.M.
Cost: Tours free; Rooms $110–$179; Romance and Pleasure Packages available
Directions: Two blocks south of Rte. 61 on Rte. 38 (Park Ave.).

FORT MADISON

By law, Fort Madison firefighters must practice for 15 minutes before they fight any fire.

Fort Madison's Santa Fe Bridge over the Mississippi River is the World's Longest Double-Deck Swing Span Bridge.

Red Men Speak with Forked Tongue

A lone statue along Muscatine's riverfront appears to honor Native Americans, but move up close and read its plaque: "Presented to the city by the Muscatine Tribe #95, Improved Order of Red Men."

Wait a second . . . *improved*? Yes, these weren't regular red men, but the "improved" ones—namely, a fraternal order of European descendants gathered "to perpetuate the beautiful legends and traditions of a vanishing race and keep alive its customs." The group started in New England as the Sons of Liberty; these were the guys who dressed as Indians and threw British tea into Boston Harbor.

After framing Native Americans for their vandalism, the Sons of Liberty renamed themselves the Improved Order of Red Men. The IORM's members have at times included George Washington, Thomas Jefferson, FDR, and Richard Nixon, though the organization was long off-limits to *real* red men. Now that the group is dying out, it does not black-ball Native Americans, though few seem interested. Can you blame them?

Riverside Park, Cedar St. and Mississippi Dr., Muscatine, IA 52761

No phone

Hours: Always visible

Cost: Free

www.redmen.org

Directions: Just south of Rte. 61 (Mississippi Dr.), crossing the railroad tracks at Chestnut St.

IOWA CITY

The butterfly swimming stroke was invented in 1935 by University of Iowa swimming coach Dave Armbruster.

The University of Iowa has the nation's largest bagpipe band.

Becky bit the dust.

Oskaloosa
Mule Cemetery

Just because you've been an ass all your life doesn't mean you're not entitled to a decent burial, or at least Daniel Nelson didn't think so. When his two Civil War mules, 34-year-old Becky and 42-year-old Jennie, died in 1888 and 1891 (respectively), he laid them to rest in a two-critter cemetery on his farm. Nelson's homestead is now a tourist attraction, and the mule cemetery is still lovingly maintained, protected by a white picket fence. It's Iowa's only mule cemetery, and one of the few in the nation.

Nelson Homestead Pioneer Farm and Craft Museum, 2294 Oxford Ave., Oskaloosa, IA 52577

(641) 672-2989

Hours: May–October, Tuesday–Saturday 10 A.M.–4:30 P.M.

Cost: Adults $4, Kids (5–16) $1

www.nelsonpioneer.org

Directions: Northeast of town on Rte. T65 (Oxford Ave.).

Keep your prayers small.

Pella
Calvary Wayside Chapel

How many angels can dance on the head of a pin? Nobody knows. But how many folks can pray in the Calvary Wayside Chapel? About eight.

This small roadside chapel was constructed in 1965 by the Mr. & Mrs. Society of the Calvary Christian Reformed Church, and open to anyone choosing to stop by. The harsh Iowa elements eventually took their toll on the structure, which was rebuilt in 1996. (The four two-seat pews are the only original pieces retained from the first building.) The chapel is open to everyone; all the Mr.'s and Mrs.'s ask is that you conduct yourself in a respectful manner while there, and that you close the door behind you when you leave. Seems fair enough.

You should know that the folk of Pella take religion very seriously. Until recently it was against the law to swim on Sunday. And if you wanted to play a game of baseball or softball on the Sabbath, it had to be organized by a church.

E. Oskaloosa St., Pella, IA 50219

Contact: Calvary Christian Reformed Church, 408 Maple St., Pella, IA 50219

(641) 628-9193

Hours: Always open

Cost: Free

Directions: On Rte. 163 Business (Oskaloosa St.), just east of Rte. 102.

The Klokkenspel

Five times a day, like clockwork (literally), ten spooky robots come to life in downtown Pella. One animatron swings a large hammer over his head while another carves away on a log with an *enormous* knife. An old man rocks back and forth with an infant in his arms while a woman nearby blots her tears with a handkerchief. A mustachioed man leans on a rifle, a woman sweeps beside a man yoked to a pair of milk pails, and two zombie-eyed children reach out to offer you a bouquet of tulips. Sound disturbing? Don't worry—it's just the Klokkenspel, Pella's mechanical salute to its Dutch heritage.

This elaborate cuckoo clock on Molengracht Plaza, which also plays a 147-bell carillon, tells the tale of how Pella was founded. Dominie Hendrick Pieter Scholte (the guy baptizing the baby) and his wife Mareah Scholte (the one crying over her broken dishes) led 800 Hollanders to Iowa in 1847. Settlers worked as blacksmiths (the man with the hammer), carved wooden shoes (the fellow with the knife), and celebrated Tulip Time every spring. And that cowboy with the rifle? None other than Wyatt Earp, who lived in Pella as a child. The Earp family home can be seen today at Pella Historical Village (714 First Street, (641) 628-2409, www.pellatuliptime.com).

Those who love all things Dutch have plenty to keep them occupied in Pella. Everywhere you turn there's another windmill, including the

135-foot Vermeer Windmill (First and Franklin Streets), the tallest working windmill in the United States. There's also a pond shaped like a wooden shoe in the Sunken Gardens (Washington and Main streets). And every year since 1935, on the second weekend in May, the town has hosted the Tulip Time Festival, where a Tulip Queen is crowned on the 65-foot-tall Tulip Toren stage.

629 Franklin St., Pella, IA 50219

(888) 746-3882 or (641) 628-2626

E-mail: pellcvb@pella.org

Hours: 11 A.M. and 1, 3, 5, and 9 P.M.

Cost: Free

www.pella.org

Directions: One-half block east of Main St. (Rte. T14) and the town square.

KALONA

Kalona was named for a famous shorthorn bull that lived here.

KEOKUK

Author **Mark Twain** lived in Keokuk from 1854 to 1856 at the Ivins House (52 Main Street, at Second Street) while working as a printer for his brother Orion. He listed himself as "Antiquarian" in the town directory they published. The Ivins House has since been replaced by a senior center; the home Twain purchased for his mother, Jane Clemens, stood at 626 High Street, but it is also gone.

Keokuk reached 118°F on July 20, 1934, the hottest temperature ever recorded in Iowa.

It's Spock-tacular!

Riverside
Future Birthplace of Captain James T. Kirk

As Trekkies everywhere can tell you—along with countless other bits of arcane information—Captain James Tiberius Kirk will be born in Iowa on March 22, 2233. The question, unanswered in the series, is *where.*

Wonder no longer: it'll be Riverside! This town's visionary population has committed itself to breeding the future commander of the starship *Enterprise*. A thankful Gene Roddenberry sent a letter (at the request of local boosters) confirming Riverside's future place in history. Until the blessed event takes place, you'll just have to marvel at the town's 20-foot-long USS *Riverside* starship, mounted on a trailer in Legion Park. There's also a concrete marker stashed behind a storefront on Main Street marking the exact spot where the infant Kirk will first greet the world two centuries from now.

Every June the town celebrates Trek Days when nerds from across the nation descend on Riverside to count down one more year on the Kirk baby clock. You are not required to wear pointy ears, but if you do, you won't look like a dork at Spockapalooza.

USS Riverside, Legion Park, Rte. 22, Riverside, IA 52327

Birthplace, 50 Main St., Riverside, IA 52327

Contact: Riverside Area Community Club, PO Box 55, Riverside, IA 52327

(319) 648-KIRK or (319) 648-3501

Hours: Always visible

Cost: Free

www.trekfest.com

Directions: East of Rte. 218 on Rte. 22 (Main St.).

IOWA STAR TREK CONNECTIONS

Riverside isn't the only Iowa community with a Star Trek connection. **Walter Koenig**, who played Ensign Chekov on the original series, graduated from Grinnell College. And actress **Kate Mulgrew**, who played Captain Kathryn Janeway, was born in Dubuque on April 29, 1955.

KNOXVILLE

A soldier-shaped plaque in the Knoxville courthouse was cast from metal recovered from the USS *Maine*.

LE CLAIRE

Every third Saturday in August the town of Le Claire challenges the town of Port Byron, Illinois, to an interstate tug-of-war known as Tug Fest. The rope they use weighs 680 pounds.

LEE COUNTY

Lee County has *two* county seats; one courthouse is in Fort Madison and the other is in Keokuk.

Hi, ho, Barbie, awayyyyyy!
Photo by author, courtesy of the Dumont Museum.

Sigourney
Open Your Own Museum

A museum doesn't necessarily have to be a logical collection of artifacts centered on a theme, such as natural history. It could be just a place to display everything an owner/curator has in his or her collection. Such is the case of

Lyle and Helen Dumont, founders of the Dumont Museum in Sigourney.

For years, Lyle collected Roy Rogers and Dale Evans records. And pedal tractors. And bicycles. And barbed wire. And farm tractors. And riding lawn mowers. And outboard motors, and license plates, and marbles, and wrenches, and toy semi-trailers, and eyeglasses, and matchbooks, and Dr. Pepper boxes, and cardboard advertisement stand-ups . . . you get the idea.

Lyle's wife, Helen, loved dolls. And teapots. And salt and pepper shakers. And Barbie dolls. Heck, *any* dolls, even Grizzly Adams, Power Rangers, and Vanilla Ice. You heard right, *Vanilla Ice.*

When Lyle retired in 1994, he and Helen had to do *something* to keep themselves occupied, so the Dumont Museum was born. The building covers 24,000 square feet, and not a square inch is empty. Toys are stacked floor to ceiling, signs hang down from the rafters, and rows of restored tractors are lined up as far as you can see. That one couple could amass so much stuff is almost too much to fathom, but the proof is right before your eyes, if you've got an hour or so to spare.

Far and away the best part of the Dumont Museum is Dale's original collection of Rogers and Evans memorabilia. The Dumonts became friends with the famous cowpokes, which opened the doors to a trove of Hollywood cowboy and cowgirl artifacts, including comic books, lunch boxes, hats, records, toy guns, clothing, posters, cookie jars, and more.

Dumont Museum, 20545 255th St., PO Box 103, Sigourney, IA 52591

(641) 622-2592

E-mail: oliver@lisco.net

Hours: May–October, Saturday–Sunday 10 A.M.–5 P.M.

Cost: Adults $5, Kids (under 12) Free

www.angelfire.com/biz5/dumont

Directions: Three miles south of town on Rte. 149, opposite Rte. V5G.

LUCAS

John L. Lewis, one-time president of the United Mine Workers of America, was born east of Lucas on February 12, 1880. The town now has a John L. Lewis Mining & Labor Museum (102 Division Street, (641) 766-6831). Lucas also celebrates his life with a John L. Lewis Festival each Labor Day weekend.

Vedic City
Maharishi University of Management

Iowa might seem like an odd location for the Maharishi Mahesh Yogi, founder of the Transcendental Meditation (or TM) movement, to start a college. The truth is, it wasn't his first choice; Washington, D.C. was. His followers wanted to show they could curb the rising crime rate in the capital using Invincible Defense Technology (see below). But after a few years without success, the Maharishi packed up his followers and headed west. The leader dismissed Washington as a "pool of mud" and equated living there to living near Chernobyl.

No argument here.

The Maharishi purchased Fairfield's bankrupt Parsons College in 1974. Though it started as Maharishi International University, this institution is known today as the Maharishi University of Management, or MUM. The centerpiece of the campus is the Golden Dome of Pure Knowledge, an empty shell filled with mattresses where students practice yogic flying, which to an outsider looks less like levitation and more like hopping around on one's knees in the lotus position. The mattresses make the landings easier.

With MUM going strong, faculty, students, and other believers in Fairfield incorporated as their own town in 2001: Vedic City. The community was designed upon the principles of Maharishi Sthapatya Veda, or "Natural Law." All buildings in town face east, nonorganic foods are banned, and the official language is Sanskrit. Vedic City even has its own currency. This combination of Natural Law elements is said to influence good health, mental clarity, and harmony. (The resulting good vibes apparently haven't been 100 percent effective; one student stabbed another in the university cafeteria in the spring of 2004.)

Who knows what the future holds for this rapidly growing faith. Perhaps magician David Copperfield could tell you; he's built a home here. There are also plans for an amusement park called Veda Land, though developers admit they're several years away from breaking ground on the project.

Maharishi University of Management, Highway 1, Vedic City, IA 52557

(800) 369-6480 or (641) 472-1110

Hours: Visitors weekends listed on Web site

Cost: Free

http://mum.edu

Directions: At the north of Fairfield on Rte. 1, north of Merrill St.

INVINCIBLE DEFENSE TECHNOLOGY

What is Invincible Defense Technology? To be technical, it's the square root of 1 percent of a given population simultaneously engaged in the practice of yogic flying. When this magic number of yogic flyers is hopping around at the same time, a cosmic tipping point is reached. Political, ethnic, and military strife evaporates, replaced by universal harmony.

Sorry you asked?

The Maharishi once offered to bring an end to the troubles plaguing Los Angeles through Invincible Defense Technology, for a low, low $2.8 million. The plan was to gather 1,000 TM practitioners to engage in yogic flying in the heart of the blighted city—90 minutes each day—and that would do the trick. When Los Angeles didn't take them up on the offer, the Maharishi ran ads in 60 different papers nationwide to offer the service to other municipalities. They're still waiting for a call.

MUSCATINE

Muscatine-based Maid-Rite became the world's first fast food franchise in 1926.

Muscatine was originally named Casey's Wood Pile.

Walcott
World's Largest Truck Stop

There are truck stops, and there are truck stops. And then there's the Iowa 80 TA Truck Stop in Walcott, a 200-acre megaplex just north of the Walcott Exit on I-80. This isn't your standard filling station with a greasy diner and a big parking lot; it's a city. Sure, they've got a Truckomat truck wash, a laundry, and several fast food outlets. But if you've lost a filling, they've also got a dental office. Need a trim? Have a seat in the barber shop. Want to take in a film? There's a movie theater. You can even relax in the Driver's Den beside a roaring fireplace—it's just like home. But in a truck stop.

This truck stop opened small at first, in 1965, founded by Bill Moon. The Moon family still owns the company, though Bill has long since departed on a heaven-bound convoy. In his honor, the Moons plan to open a Trucking Hall of Fame here in 2005. The museum will honor trucking greats—who do you think will be the first inductee?—and be the permanent home for Bill's collection of trucks and truckabilia.

Iowa 80 TA Truck Stop, I-80 and Exit 284, Walcott, IA 52773

(563) 468-5519

Hours: Always open

Cost: Free

www.walcotttruckersjamboree.com

Directions: On the north side of I-80 at Exit 284.

West Des Moines
First Kid on a Milk Carton

Twelve-year-old Johnny Gosch has the sad distinction of being the first child ever pictured as missing on the side of a milk carton. He was last seen at 6 A.M. on September 5, 1982, while delivering newspapers on Marcourt Lane, a quiet street in West Des Moines. Minutes later he was gone.

Anderson Erikson Dairy, a local milk bottler, placed Johnny's picture on its cartons, asking for leads in the case. Unfortunately, no leads ever panned out; Gosch has never been found. But the idea of placing children's faces on milk cartons caught on, with some success.

There is a downside to the proliferation of milk carton campaigns, however: the ever-present sense of lurking doom that has seeped into the nation's consciousness. Stranger danger! But is it warranted? Law enforcement officials admit that nine times out of ten (and more, according to some studies), the child you see on a carton is not dead or physically harmed, but living with an estranged parent. Knowing this is not to dismiss the need to locate these missing children, but to better understand the nature of the problem: the faces on milk cartons are not being kidnapped by strangers, by and large, but are being used as emotional pawns in bitter custody battles. In other words: the danger is a little closer to home.

Marcourt Lane and 42nd St., West Des Moines, IA 50266

No phone

Hours: Always visible

Cost: Free

Directions: One block north of Ashworth Rd. on 42nd St.

OTTUMWA

Richard Nixon was the legal officer at the U.S. Naval Air Station in Ottumwa from 1942 to 1943. Pat Nixon worked as a teller at the Union Bank & Trust Company. The couple lived in the Hillside Apartments at Green and E. Fourth Streets.

Novelist **Edna Ferber** lived in Ottumwa as a child at 410 N. Wapello Street, between 1890 and 1897. She recalled, "I don't think there was a day when I wasn't called a sheeny."

If a man wants to wink at a woman in Ottumwa, he must know her first.

COURT-SANCTIONED KIDNAPPING?

Not every child who gets snatched from his or her parents ends up on a milk carton. On February 10, 1991, single mother Clara Clausen of Cedar Rapids gave up her two-day-old daughter, and the girl's (supposed) biologic father, Scott Seefeldt, signed the papers as well. The girl was adopted by Jan and Roberta DeBoer of Ann Arbor, Michigan, who named her Jessica.

But Seefeldt wasn't Jessica's biologic father; a man named Dan Schmidt was. Clausen and Schmidt had broken up shortly after Clausen had gotten pregnant, and Clausen never told Schmidt of her predicament. Less than a month after Jessica was gone, however, the pair had second thoughts, and filed a petition to get the child back. After six months of genetic testing, an Iowa court nullified the adoption papers signed by Seefeldt and ordered that Jessica be returned to Cedar Rapids.

Not so fast, the DeBoers said. Before the Iowa Supreme Court they questioned Schmidt's fitness as a parent; he'd previously fathered two other children, each by a different mother, and wasn't supporting either of them. To show what kind of parents they could be, Schmidt and Clausen got married in April 1992 . . . as if that settled anything.

In December 1992 the Iowa Supreme Court ruled 8-to-1 in favor of the Schmidts. The DeBoers appealed to a Michigan judge on grounds of improper jurisdiction, and he ruled in their favor. The Schmidts took the case to the Michigan Court of Appeals, which sided with them. The DeBoers appealed to the Michigan Supreme Court, but it also sided with the Schmidts. The Supreme Court refused to hear any appeal, so on August 2, 1993, while most of America watched in horror on TV, a crying Jessica was returned to Cedar Rapids.

Whichever side you might agree with, it's hard to forgive the glacial pace at which the many courts ruled in this custody battle, ultimately deciding the case of a one-month-old at the age of thirty months.

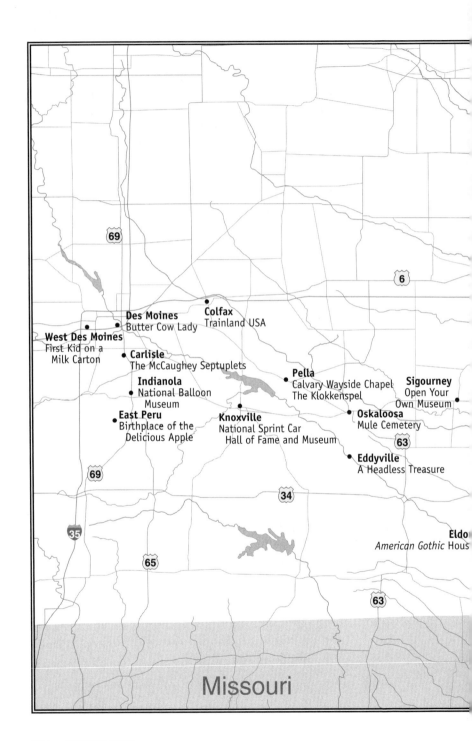

Iowa City
Death to Non-Virgins!

West Branch
Herbert Hoover
Presidential Library

Walcott
World's Largest Truck Stop

Montpelier
Varner's Caboose

Davenport
The Brady Street Banshee
The Davenport Stone
Mother Goose in a Zoo
Palmer College

Riverside
Future Birthplace
of Captain James T. Kirk

Muscatine
Pearl Button Museum
Phantasuite Hotel
Red Men Speak
with Forked Tongue

Columbus Junction
Lovers Leap Bridge

Fruitland
World's Largest
Watermelon Slice

Vedic City
Maharishi University of Management

Lockridge
Johnny Clock Museum

Burlington
Snake Alley

Illinois

5

CELEBRITIES IN TROUBLE TOUR

*F*or reasons that are not entirely clear, Iowa has spelled the end of the road (or the last wrong turn just before the end of the road) for a number of celebrities. You probably already know what happened to Buddy Holly, Ritchie Valens, and the Big Bopper, but were you aware that Rocky Marciano and Cary Grant also drew their last breaths in the Hawkeye State? Bonnie and Clyde nearly bought the farm in a hail of bullets, as did Anita Bryant's career, but in her case it was in a single volley of banana cream pie. Only Tom Arnold, Ozzy Osbourne, and Howard Dean were able to bounce back from their Iowa difficulties, and none of them bounced back all that far.

The purpose of this special Celebrities in Trouble Tour is not to revel in others' misfortune—except, of course, Anita Bryant's—but to provide nine cautionary tales for any celebrity who might pick up this guidebook. Non-famous readers can draw whatever lesson they'd like.

Cedar Rapids
The Birth of Bad

When the Cherry sisters of Marion—Addie, Jessie, Effie, and occasionally Lizzie—decided to go into show business, they didn't let a little thing like lack of talent get in their way. The horrid show they created was a conglomeration of one-act morality plays, patriotic ballads, bad poetry, and interpretive dance, sometimes accompanied by a yipping dog. Audiences routinely greeted the Cherrys with overripe tomatoes, peach pits, and rotten eggs. Still, suffering for one's art has its limits, so Addie took to brandishing a shotgun on stage.

Newspaper reviews were mixed. Some focused on the sisters' performances: ". . . [if they didn't know] they were acting the parts of monkeys, it does seem like the overshoes thrown at them would convey the idea." Others talked about the sisters' stage presence: "Jessie narrowly escaped being pretty; the others were never in such danger." The Cherrys poo-pooed their detractors as a ranting gaggle of jealous no-talents, which certainly could have been true. But the showers of rotten vegetables? The patrons were put up to it by the theater owners, the women hypothesized.

They were probably right about that. With the reputation as the "World's Worst Sister Act" preceding them, the Cherrys were enthusiastically booked all over Iowa to packed vaudeville houses. Theater owners took to installing chicken wire between the stage and the seats for safety's sake, though it probably wasn't necessary; if reports of their performances can be trusted, the Cherrys did have one talent: dodging projectiles.

By 1896 word of the Cherrys' act reached New York and the struggling Oscar Hammerstein, whose Olympia Music Hall had him in debt to his eyeballs. He immediately hired the sisters and brought them to the Big Apple. The Cherrys' *Something Good, Something Sad* opened on Broadway on November 16 to critical disdain. Jessie belted out "Fair Columbia" while draped in an American flag. Effie played the romantic lead in a sketch titled "The Gypsy's Warning" and was corrupted by a ne'er-do-well Don Juan, as portrayed by Addie. Jessie banged incessantly on a bass drum through many of the musical numbers, so when she was crucified during the "Clinging to the Cross" living-sculpture tableau, the audience was delighted.

Actually, the crowd *loved* every minute of the sisters' performance. A reviewer observed the audience "never missed a note, or found one either." The Cherrys played for ten weeks to standing-room-only crowds, and

Hammerstein was able to fend off his creditors.

Over the next seven years, the Cherrys toured the United States and Canada. Following an Iowa performance in 1898, Billy Hamilton, editor of the *Odebolt Chronicle*, wrote a scathing review that said, in part, "The mouths of their rancid features opened like caverns, and sounds like the wailing of damned souls issued therefrom."

Enough was enough. The sisters sued the *Des Moines Leader* (where the review had been reprinted) for $15,000. The case made it to the Iowa Supreme Court in 1901 where the justices ruled that a reviewer could critique a public performance without fear of libel, even if the review was harsh or extreme, which in this case it probably wasn't. The case established a legal precedent that protects reviewers to this day.

Jessie died in 1903 of typhoid fever, and the remaining sisters returned to their family farm in Marion. The Cherrys' less-talented sister Ella had maintained the homestead while the rest were on the road. When their savings dried up, the sisters sold the farm and moved to Cedar Rapids where they opened a bakery. Effie ran for mayor of Cedar Rapids in 1924 and 1926, but she was no more of a politician than she was a singer. She once threatened voters, "Ankle-length skirts will be the style if I have my way!" Effie lost handily. The sisters tried several comeback tours, but lightning and tomatoes don't strike twice.

When the last of the sisters, Effie, died in 1944, the *New York Times* wrote, "Maybe the Cherry sisters knew better than the public did what was really going on. Be this as it may, they left behind an imperishable memory. And they gave more pleasure to their audiences than did many a performer who was merely almost good." Effie was buried beside her sister Addie at the Linwood Cemetery in Cedar Rapids. Ellie and Lizzie are planted at the Oak Shade Cemetery in Marion. A small display on the Cherry Sisters can be found at the History Center in their old hometown.

The History Center, 615 First Ave. SE, Cedar Rapids, IA 52401

(319) 362-1501

E-mail: leeann@historycenter.org

Hours: Tuesday–Wednesday and Friday–Saturday 10 A.M.–4 P.M., Thursday 10 A.M.–7 P.M., Sunday Noon–4 P.M.

Cost: Adults $4, Seniors (62+) $3.25, Kids (6–17) $2

www.historycenter.org or www.rootsweb.com/~iaohms/cherrysisters.html

Directions: Downtown at the corner of Sixth St. and First Ave. SE.

Dexter
Bonnie and Clyde—Ambushed!

On July 23, 1933, a posse intent on capturing or killing Bonnie and Clyde ambushed their five-member gang in a park along the banks of the South Raccoon River, just north of Dexter, Iowa. The early morning shootout left Marvin "Buck" Barrow (Clyde's brother) near death and his wife, Blanche, in custody. Buck was shot twice, but he had already been mortally wounded in an earlier gun battle in Platte City, Missouri; witnesses in Dexter reported that his brains were oozing out of a week-old hole in his skull. Buck died of pneumonia in the King's Daughters Hospital in Perry six days later. Blanche had also been injured in Missouri when shattering glass hit her in the eyes, though she was well enough to be thrown into the Dallas County Jail in Adel. She was soon transferred to the Polk County Jail in Des Moines, when officials feared her at-large cohorts might attempt a rescue.

Both Bonnie and Clyde escaped that morning, along with accomplice W. D. Jones, though all sustained gunshot wounds. The trio kidnapped farmer Valley Fellers just north of the river, along with his son Marvelle and hired hand Walter Spillers. They drove Fellers's car through Redfield to Polk City, where it was abandoned and the men released. The events of that day only enhanced Bonnie and Clyde's reputation as uncatchable. They had eluded 150 armed men! Locals later confessed that the posse had gotten drunk the night *before* their morning raid. (Note to future posses: capture first, party later.)

Rumors have long circulated around Dexter that the gang buried some of their booty the night before the gun battle. Since they weren't able to recover the loot during their hasty escape, it might still be there. Good luck trying to find it.

Dexfield Park, Dexfield Rd., Dexter, IA 50070

No phone

Hours: Always visible

Cost: Free

http://texashideout.tripod.com/Dexfield.html

Directions: Head north out of town on Rte. P48 (Dexfield Rd.) until it bends to the left; the park was in the field to the right, just south of the river.

Clear Lake and Mason City
The Day the Music Died

What day did the music die? February 3, 1959. Buddy Holly, Ritchie Valens, and J. P. "The Big Bopper" Richardson's chartered plane crashed into a frozen Iowa soybean field, bringing at least two promising careers to an early end.

The trio had come to Clear Lake's Surf Ballroom on their Winter Dance Party tour. The next stop was Moorhead, Minnesota, and nobody was looking forward to the ride on the cold tour bus. Holly chartered a plane from the Dwyer Flying Service to fly ahead to Fargo, North Dakota (the closest airport to Moorhead), with the group's costumes in order to get them laundered for the next gig.

Before leaving for the Mason City Airport, Holly and Valens called home from a pay phone in the Surf's lobby. The phone still hangs in the Surfside 6 Café in this recently restored venue, which hosts a Winter Dance Party each February in memoriam.

The Surf Ballroom, 460 N. Shore Dr., Clear Lake, IA 50428

(641) 357-6151

E-mail: thesurf@netins.net

Hours: Monday–Friday 9 A.M.–4 P.M., and for shows

Cost: Free; Tours $4

www.surfballroom.com

Directions: South on Eighth St. from Rte. 18, right on First Ave., then right on Shore Dr. to Buddy Holly Pl.

There were two open seats on the Beechcraft Bonanza, in addition to Holly's and the pilot's. J. P. Richardson had the flu and wanted to see a doctor, so Waylon Jennings (who played bass guitar in Holly's band) gave up his seat. Valens won his short ride in a coin toss with Tommy Allsup, also from Holly's band.

At the airport, Holly ribbed Jennings, "I hope your bus freezes up."

"Well, I hope your plane crashes," Jennings replied.

Mason City Airport, Highway 18W, PO Box 1484, Mason City, IA 50401

(641) 421-3680

E-mail: posgood@netconx.net

Hours: Always visible

Cost: Free

www.masoncity.net/departments/Airport%20Commission/index.php?dept=
Airport%20Commission

Directions: Just east of I-35 on the north side of Rte. 18/122 (265th St.).

The place the music died.

Roger Peterson, the 21-year-old pilot, had no experienced with winter flying conditions, and it showed. He slammed his plane into a field only five miles northwest of the airport. When the foursome failed to land in

North Dakota, a search party was organized. The twisted wreckage was found the next day along a fence line on the farm of Albert Juhl. The plane had hit the ground at full throttle. Holly's trademark glasses weren't found until 21 years after the crash, unearthed by a farmer's plow.

Today a small marker along the fence marks the spot where the plane came to rest. The farm's current owner allows fans to go onto his land to see the marker, but asks that visitors follow the fence line from the main road and not trample his crops.

Gull Ave. and 315th St., Mason City, IA 50401

No phone

Hours: Daylight hours

Cost: Free

Directions: From the intersection of Rte. 18 and Eighth St. in Clear Lake, head north on Eighth/Grouse Ave. (Rte. S28) for 4.7 miles until just before the road turns to the left. Turn right onto the dirt road, 310th St., then left (north) at the next intersection onto Gull Ave. Park near the intersection of Gull Ave. and 315th St. and walk west into the field along the south side of the fence. The marker is about a half-mile ahead, just past the fence line running north–south.

Newton
The Day the Boxer Died

As you've just read, Iowa's winters can be rather unforgiving to inexperienced pilots of light aircraft. Iowa's summer thunderstorms aren't much friendlier.

Boxer Rocky Marciano was visiting Chicago on August 31, 1969, and was planning to return to his home in Fort Lauderdale, Florida, to attend his daughter's sweet sixteen birthday party. But before he did, Marciano made a promise to his friend Frank Farrell to attend a fight in Des Moines. There was just enough time for Marciano and Farrell to fly to Iowa and watch the bout, then return to the Windy City for a flight home the next day. The pair hired rookie pilot Glenn Belz to take them to Des Moines, unaware that Belz was not instrument-rated and had only logged 35 hours at night.

The trio left Chicago's Midway Airport despite reports of thunderstorms and a low cloud ceiling around Des Moines. Pilot Belz called air traffic control in Des Moines to ask for help finding and landing at Newton Municipal Airport, which was blanketed with clouds. The Cessna Skyhawk popped through the ceiling two miles short of the runway, clipped a lone oak tree in a cornfield, and crashed. All three men died on impact. Marciano was only 45 years old.

Newton Municipal Airport, Rte. S74, Newton, IA 50208

(641) 792-1292

Hours: Always visible

Cost: Free

Directions: The plane crashed in a field two miles due south of the airport.

Des Moines
"At least it wasn't fruitcake."

Call it Soopy Sales activism. On October 14, 1977, orange juice spokeswoman Anita Bryant was expanding her Florida antigay crusade to the Midwest, and was holding a press conference in Des Moines. While she prattled on, a "journalist" stepped forward and hit her in the face with a banana cream pie. The thrower turned out to be local activist Tom Higgins, who had posed as a reporter to get into the event. (Question: how does one sneak a pie past security?)

While wiping banana goo from her face, Bryant tried to laugh it off, observing, "At least it wasn't fruitcake." Unable to contain her emotions, she burst out crying, and the press conference ground to a halt. In the months that followed, so did her career.

Given the buckets of tears shed by the victims of Bryant's virulent homophobic campaign, her bawling didn't garner much sympathy. And as far as her career was concerned, it's worth remembering that her Save Our Children campaign was aimed at ending the chosen careers of many gays and lesbians across Florida. Call it karma.

Anita Bryant must have known there was a pie out there with her name on it, though she probably never expected it to be delivered in Iowa. Surprise!

Marsden/American Security Corporation (former offices of Iowa Public Television), 2801 Bell Ave., Des Moines, IA 50321

No phone

Hours: Always visible

Cost: Free

Directions: Head north three blocks on 30th St. from Park Ave., then east on Bell Ave.

Ottumwa
Tom Arnold Escapes

Tom Arnold was on a fast track to Loserville in the early 1980s, and had he not spotted Andy Kaufman outside Ottumwa's Jailhouse bar, he might have ended up in a real jailhouse. Kaufman had been visiting Maharishi University in nearby Fairfield, but had been lured away by an ad for a female oil-wrestling contest being held at the Coliseum (102 Church Street, (641) 683-0675). But that's getting ahead of the story. . . .

The Arnold family of Ottumwa put the fun in dysfunctional. Tom's childhood and adolescence is described in embarrassing (and surprisingly entertaining) detail in his memoir, *How I Lost 5 Pounds in 6 Years*. Tom was born here in on March 6, 1959. His mother left the family when Tom was four years old. She was granted custody of Tom in a bitter 1963 divorce, but relinquished him a day after the settlement because he cramped her style. She would go on to marry six more times before she turned 35. Tom attended Anne G. Wilson Elementary (1102 E. Fourth Street, (641) 684-5441) where he told his new kindergarten teacher that his family's home on Center Street had burned to the ground. After Tom received both sympathy and gifts, the teacher learned that there had been no fire, and alerted the media. The local newspaper ran a front-page story titled "The Little Boy Who Told the Big Lie." Ouch.

This was just the beginning of his troubles. Arnold was busted for spray painting his name on Ottumwa's Memorial Park water tower. He was arrested at age 16 for stealing a stop sign, though never caught for running over 35 others. And he was eventually kicked out of the house for throwing a party while the rest of his family was away on vacation. After high school he worked days at the local Hormel meatpacking plant where he "chiseled" the heads of pigs, and at night attended Indian Hills Community College (525 Grandview Avenue, (800) 726-2585).

Then, in 1980, Arnold was arrested for streaking through the Jefferson Square Manor retirement home and, later, Mr. Quick's restaurant downtown. With nothing left to hide, he came up with a novel idea to raise money for tuition: he announced a one-person, all-but-nude walk-a-thon dubbed "From Here to There in Underwear." "Here" was Albia and "there" was Ottumwa, a distance of about 25 miles. The fundraiser, which took place in 9-degree weather in the dead of winter, helped Arnold raise $3,000 for college.

As you might suspect, Arnold never finished his studies. After meeting Andy Kaufman outside the Jailhouse, he followed the comedian to the Coliseum. After the matches, Kaufman took the wrestlers, Arnold, and the fans—250 in all—to Happy Joe's for free burgers. By the end of the night, Arnold knew what he wanted to do with his life, and it didn't involve Ottumwa: he would be a comedian.

Happy Joe's, 315 Church St., Ottumwa, IA 52501

(641) 682-4565

Hours: Sunday–Friday 11 A.M.–9 P.M., Saturday 11 A.M.–10 P.M.

Cost: Free; Meals, $6–$10

www.happyjoes.com

Directions: Head two blocks southwest of Rte. 34 on Jefferson St., then cut northwest one block to Church St., which is one-way heading northeast; one block ahead.

YOU SHOULDN'T GO HOME AGAIN

After **Tom Arnold** married **Roseanne Barr** in the early 1990s, they decided to build a $3+ million getaway on a 1,700-acre spread near Eldon. Because there wasn't a restaurant in town open past 6:30 P.M., the couple opened Roseanne and Tom's Big Food Diner (101 Elm Street). It specialized in loose-meat sandwiches, better known as Maid-Rites. The walls were filled with the couple's autographed photo collection and mementos from the ill-fated *Jackie Thomas Show*. When the pair broke up in 1995, the diner was closed and construction halted on their mansion. Unable to agree on who would get what, they donated the half-finished building to Indian Hills Community College. The diner was eventually bulldozed.

Please don't eat the bats.

Des Moines
Ozzy Osbourne Bat-Biting Site

Two decades before he was reintroduced to the TV-viewing public as a doddering, confused father figure, Ozzy Osbourne toured the world as the self-proclaimed Prince of Darkness. As part of his 1981–82 "Blizzard of Oz" tour, Ozzy would thrill the audience by biting the heads off rubber bats that his roadies tossed at him. Unfortunately, somebody at a Des Moines show tossed a *real* bat onto the stage where, on concert autopilot, Ozzy picked it up and bit off its head.

He realized the mistake immediately but, like any true performer, went on with the show. After the final encore, Osbourne was taken to a local hospital, where he began treatment for a potential rabies infection.

Wait a second—what kind of "Prince of Darkness" gets a vaccination?

Veterans Memorial Auditorium, 833 Fifth Ave., Des Moines, IA 50309

(515) 242-2946

E-mail: vets@co.polk.ia.us

Hours: Always visible

Cost: Free

www.vetsauditorium.com

Directions: Three blocks south of I-235 on Fifth Ave., four block west of the river.

Davenport
Cary Grant's Death Site

Cary Grant led a fairly glamorous life and probably never expected to die in a Davenport hospital. However, that's just what happened. Grant came to Davenport to appear in a production titled "A Conversation with Cary Grant" (the perfect role!). On November 29, 1986, he was finishing an afternoon rehearsal at the Adler Theatre (136 E. Third Street, (563) 326-8555) when he became lightheaded, so he returned to his dressing room to sit down. Not feeling any better, he went back to his suite at the Blackhawk Hotel (200 E. Third Street, (563) 328-8000) with his wife, Barbara Harris.

Grant didn't know it at the time, but he had suffered a massive stroke. Later in the evening he started vomiting and was taken by ambulance to St. Luke's Hospital. Grant arrived in a coma and died shortly before midnight. He was 82.

Genesis Health Systems (former St. Luke's Hospital), 1401 W. Central Park Ave.,

Davenport, IA 52804

(563) 421-1000

Hours: Always visible

Cost: Free

www.genesishealth.com

Directions: Twelve blocks south of Rte. 6, five blocks east of Division St.

DES MOINES

Paul Gray, the bass player for the band Slipknot, ran a red light in Des Moines on June 1, 2003, and struck another car. Police found cocaine and marijuana in his vehicle, and arrested Gray.

Maybe next time--yeeeeeeehaaaaaaawwwww!!!!!!!

West Des Moines
Howard Dean: I Have a Scream

It was the scream heard round the world . . . over and over and over and over and over and over again. After coming in a disappointing third in the Iowa Democratic Caucus on January 20, 2004, Vermont Governor Howard Dean (the long-reported front-runner for the Democratic nomination) took the stage at the Val Air Ballroom and tried to pump up his demoralized troops. "We will not quit now or ever! We will win our country back for ordinary Americans! And we are going to win Massachusetts and North Carolina and Missouri and Arkansas and Connecticut and New York and Ohio. . . . " he shouted, his face crimson. And then he capped off his list of states with the scream you've no doubt heard but couldn't reproduce if you tried.

"Is he nuts?" the media wondered aloud, day after day after day after day after day.

No, he wasn't nuts. Passionate? Yes. But unbalanced? Oh, please. With so much cynicism surrounding American politics, why is a candidate's enthusiasm automatically suspect?

Though it turned out to be the beginning of the end for Dean's presidential bid, it was hardly a defeat. Quite the contrary. By the time he bellowed his fateful screech, Dean and his idealistic supporters had reenergized the Democratic Party, which nearly unseated George Bush in 2004. Dean may have lost the battle, but the war? Look out 2008!

Val Air Ballroom, 301 Ashworth Rd., West Des Moines, IA 50265

(515) 223-6152

Hours: Always visible

Cost: Free

www.valairballroom.com

Directions: One block west of Rte. 28 on Ashworth Rd., one block north of Grand Ave.; Rte. 28 is 63rd St. in Des Moines, but First St. in West Des Moines.

EPiLOGUE

*N*ow comes the bad news: Iowa's unique roadside attractions are an endangered species. After reading this book you're probably thinking these oddities are common . . . but you'd be wrong.

Need proof? Mason City was once home to an accordion-shaped diner owned by bandleader Lawrence Welk. Its specialty was the Squeezeburger. It *was* the Squeezeburger, not *is*—both the diner and the burgers (and Lawrence Welk, for that matter) are gone. Ottumwa had a Coal Palace with a 200-foot-tall tower. Yep, *had*, not has. The Jesse James Museum in Adair might as well have been robbed, because it no longer exists. The same goes for the Flood Museum in Fort Madison, washed away by the rising waters of tourist indifference. Iowa City Wonderland is now Iowa City Never-Never Land, Mason City's Van Horn Antique Truck Museum has been hauled away, and just try to find a giant Happy Chef statue to talk to—those guys used to be everywhere, but not anymore.

Not all of Iowa's long-gone attractions fell victim to apathy. Blame a few demises on lawyers and bureaucrats. The folks of Decorah decided to seal up their Ice Cave because—I kid you not—they were worried visitors might injure themselves by slipping . . . *on the ice.* In the Ice Cave. Well, duh! And a few citizens in Waverly wanted to erect a Big Chicken, but were hampered by City Hall. The mayor probably thought there were more pressing civic concerns, though what those issues could be escapes a person like me.

While working on this book I drove to what was once the Maquoketa Caves Nature Center, only to find its doors sealed shut, probably forever. Inside I knew there was a stuffed two-headed calf and a lamb with two butts, and that I wouldn't be able to see either of them. This depressed me more than it should have, but it still depressed me. If you want to see the Hobo Museum, or the Albino Deer, or the Future Birthplace of Captain James T. Kirk, I suggest that you do it before it's too late. You don't want to find yourself like I did, in the middle of nowhere, map in hand, cursing the cultural darkness.

I'm talking about *this weekend*. Those projects you've been meaning to get to—the uncleaned gutters, the laundry room that needs painting, that sibling you've been meaning to call—they'll all still be there next week. But the World's Largest Cheeto? I make no guarantees.

ACKNOWLEDGMENTS

$\mathbb{S}$ome of my fondest childhood memories were of family trips to Iowa. My grandparents lived in Alton (my father was born in Linn Grove), and my Uncle Alvin and Aunt Sue had a farm north of Sibley: Oleo Acres, "One of the Cheaper Spreads." As a kid, I thought the farm was one of the greatest places on earth; my brothers and I got to ride go-carts and snowmobiles, walk the beans, play daredevil in the hay mow, and see chickens, cows, and pigs up close.

I still love Iowa and the folks who live in, and come from, the Hawk-eye State. I am fortunate to have met hundreds of Iowans in my life, and though a few turned out to be ornery cusses, I've never met an Iowa jerk. Not one. That says a lot about the state. And as for scenery, I challenge anyone to show me anything as beautiful as a field of Iowa corn in August.

This book would not have been possible without the assistance, patience, and good humor of many individuals. My thanks go out to the following people for allowing me to interview them about their roadside attractions: Patrick Acton (Matchstick Marvels), Fred Archer (Archer Engines of Yesteryear), Robert Birkby (Fremont County Historical Museum Complex), Fern Carlson (Country Relics Village), Bev Champan (International Wrestling Institute and Museum), Lyle Dumont (Dumont Museum), Gwen Ecklund (Donna Reed Foundation), Jeanne (Jefferson Telephone Company Museum), Mick Jurgensen (The Big Treehouse), Dennis Laughlin (Battle Hill Museum of Natural History), Darwin Linn (Villisca Ax Murder House), John McLain (Johnny Clock Museum), Tom Straub (Sister Sarah's), Mr. Weesner (Bonnie and Clyde in Dexter), and Chuck Welch (Twister House).

For research assistance, I am indebted to the librarians in the Iowa communities of Adair, Algona, Cedar Rapids, Clarinda, Council Bluffs, Davenport, Denison, Des Moines, Emmetsburg, Estherville, Fort Dodge, Glidden, Guttenberg, Jefferson, Laurens, Mason City, Muscatine, Onawa, Ottumwa, Pella, Sioux City, Villisca, Waterloo, Webster City, and Winterset. Thanks also to the Visitors Bureaus and/or Chambers of Commerce in Ames, Anamosa, Arnolds Park, Audubon, Belle Plaine, Boone, Britt, Burlington, Cedar Falls, Cedar Rapids, Clarinda, Clear Lake, Council Bluffs, Creston, Davenport, Decorah, Denison, Des Moines, Dubuque, Dyersville, Elk Horn, Ida Grove, Indianola, Iowa City, Jefferson, Kimballton, Knoxville, Le Mars, Logan, Marshalltown, Mason City, Muscatine, New Hampton, Newton, Onawa, Pella, Riverside, St. Ansgar, Shenandoah, Sioux City, Spillville, Stanton, Storm Lake, Strawberry Point, Tama, Traer, Waterloo, West Branch, and Winterset.

Thank you John McLain and Wayne Kauffman, for posing in my photographs, and Dana Brown and Denise Troxell, for your hospitality. To my Iowa and Iowa-born friends: Bob Brown, Debbie, Bill and Jen, all the folks at the Davenport ACT office, I hope you enjoy the book.

Many thanks (as always) to everyone at IPG and Chicago Review Press—half of whom seem to have attended Grinnell—for your continuing support of the Oddball travel series, particularly Cynthia Sherry (also a Grinnell grad). Thank you, Allison Felus, for editing this book, and Gerilee Hundt, High Priestess of Production. And lastly, to Jim Frost, my deepest appreciation for being there from the beginning.

RECOMMENDED SOURCES

If you'd like to learn more about the places and individuals in this book, the following are excellent sources.

Iowa (General)

The Great Iowa Touring Book by Mike Whye (Black Earth, WI: Trails Books, 2004)

Iowa Off the Beaten Path, 4th Edition by Lori Erickson (Old Saybrook, CT: Globe Pequot Press, 1999)

Great Iowa Weekend Adventures by Mike Whye (Black Earth, WI: Trails Books, 2001)

Iowa (History)

A Treasury of Iowa Tales by Webb Garrison (Nashville, TN: Rutledge Hill Press, 2000)

Iowa Historical Tour Guide, 2nd Edition by D. Ray Wilson (Carpentersville, IL: Crossroads Communications, 1991.)

Iowa Pride by Duane A. Schmidt (Ames, IA: Iowa State University Press, 1996)

Rogues and Heroes from Iowa's Amazing Past by George Mills (Ames, IA: Iowa State University Press, 1972)

Iowa's Historical Markers by Virginia Roth and Ardis McMechan (Ames, IA: Nite Owl Printing, 1998)

Iowa (Trivia)

Amazing Iowa by Janice Beck Stock (Nashville, TN: Rutledge Hill Press, 2003)

Iowa Trivia by Janice B. Stock, Alan Beck, and Ken Beck (Nashville, TN: Rutledge Hill Press, 1996)

Iowa (Ghosts)

Ghostly Tales of Iowa by Ruth D. Hein and Vicky L. Hinsenbrock (Ames, IA: Iowa State University Press, 1996)

1. Northwest Iowa

Jesse James

Jesse James: The Man and the Myth by Marley Brant (New York: Berkley Books, 1998)

Jesse James: Last Rebel of the Civil War by T. J. Stiles (New York: Vintage, 2002)

The Spirit Lake Massacre

The Spirit Lake Massacre by Bob Brown (Spirit Lake, IA: Self-published, Date unknown)

Hoboes

Hobo: A Young Man's Thoughts on Trains and Tramping in America by Eddie Joe Cotton (New York: Three Rivers Press, 2003)

Done and Been: Steel Rail Chronicles of American Hobos by Gypsy Moon (Bloomington, IN: Indiana University Press, 1996)

Donna Reed

In Search of Donna Reed by Jay Fultz (Iowa City, IA: University of Iowa Press, 2001)

Winnebagoes

Home on the Road: The Motor Home in America by Roger B. White (Washington, DC: Smithsonian Institution Press, 2000)

The Cardiff Giant

The Cardiff Giant: A Hundred Year Old Hoax by Barbara Franco (Cooperstown, NY: New York State Historical Association, 1990)

The Original Cardiff Giant by Alan Hynd (Fort Dodge, IA: Fort Dodge Historical Museum, Fort, and Stockade, 1951)

The Straight Story

The Straight Story by John Roach and Mary Sweeney (New York: Hyperion, 1999) (Screenplay)

Kate Shelley, Train Saver

Kate Shelley and the Midnight Express by Margaret K. Wetterer (Minneapolis, MN: Carolrhoda Books, 1990) (Children's title)

The Crash of Flight 232
Chosen to Live by Kevin Schemmel (Littleton, CO: Victory Publishing Company, 1996)

Ann Landers and Dear Abby
Dear Ann, Dear Abby by Jan Pottker and Bob Speziale (New York: Dodd, Mead & Company, 1987)

Witch Hunt
Sex-Crime Panic: A Journey to the Paranoid Heart of the 1950s by Neil Miller (Los Angeles: Alyson Books, 2002)

Grotto of the Redemption
Grotto Father by Duane Hutchinson (Lincoln, NE: Foundation Books, 1989)
A Pictorial Story of the Grotto of the Redemption by Father Louis H. Greving (West Bend, IA: Grotto of the Redemption, 1993)
An Explanation of the Grotto of the Redemption by Father Paul Dobberstein (West Bend, IA: Grotto of the Redemption, date unknown)
Backyard Visionaries: Grassroots in the Midwest by Barbara Brackman and Cathy Dwigans (Lawrence, KS: University Press of Kansas, 1999)

2. Northeast Iowa
Laura Ingalls Wilder and the Little Hotel in the Village
Laura: The Life of Laura Ingalls Wilder by Donald Zochert (New York: Avon Books, 1976)
The Little House Guidebook by William Anderson (New York: HarperTrophy, 1996)

World's Smallest Church
Souvenir Folder of the World's Smallest Church near Festina, Iowa (Festina, IA: Self-published, date unknown)

Bil Baird
Bil Baird . . . He Pulled Lots of Strings by Richard Leet (Mason City, IA: Charles H. MacNider Museum, 1988)

The Music Man
Meredith Willson: The Unsinkable Music Man by John C. Skipper (Mason City, IA: Savas Publishing Company, 2000)

Maytag Washing Machines
The Spirit of Maytag by the Maytag Corporation (Newton, IA: The Maytag Corporation, date unknown)

The Bily Clocks
Bily Brothers: Wood Carvers and Clock Makers by Duane Hutchinson (Lincoln, NE: Foundation Books, 1993)
The Bily Clocks by Anonymous (Spillville, IA: Self-published, date unknown)

The Sullivan Brothers
We Band of Brothers: The Sullivans & World War II by John Satterfield (Parkersburg, IA: Mid-Prairie Books, 1995)

Herbert Hoover
The Presidency of Herbert C. Hoover by Martin L. Fausold (Lawrence, KS: University Press of Kansas, 1988)

3. Southwest Iowa

Glenn Miller
Chattanooga Choo Choo: The Life and Times of the World Famous Glenn Miller Orchestra by Richard Grudens (New York: Celebrity Profiles, 2004)

Johnny Carson
King of the Night by Laurence Leamer (New York: Morrow, 1989)

The Villisca Ax Murders
Villisca by Roy Marshall (Chula Vista, CA: Aventine Press, 2003)
"Midwest Nightmares" in *With an Axe* by H. Paul Jeffers (New York: Pinnacle Books, 2000)

John Wayne
John Wayne by Randy Roberts and James S. Olson (New York: Free Press, 1995)

The Bridges of Madison County
The Bridges of Madison County by Robert James Waller (New York: Warner Books, 1992)

4. Southeast Iowa

The McCaughey Septuplets

Seven from Heaven by Kenny and Bobbi McCaughey (Nashville, TN: Thomas Nelson Publishers, 1998)

The Davenport Stone

"Iowa's Davenport Stone: 19th Century Hoax or 2,000-year-old Artifact?" by James Grimes (*Ancient American*, Volume 4, Issue 28)

Palmer College

Old Dad Chiro: A Biography of D. D. Palmer Founder of Chiropractic by Vern Gielow (La Crosse, WI: Barge Chiropractic Publishing, 1995)

The Butter Cow Lady and the State Fair

The Butter Cow Lady: The Story of Norma "Duffy" Lyon by B. Green (Des Moines, IA: Target Publishing, 1998)

The American State Fair by Derek Nelson (Osceola, WI: MBI Publishing Company, 1999)

Grant Wood and American Gothic

Grant Wood and Little Sister Nan by Julie Jensen McDonald (Iowa City, IA: Penfield Press, 2000)

Grant Wood: An American Master Revealed by Brady M. Roberts, et al (San Francisco, CA: Pomegranate Books, 1995)

5. Celebrities in Trouble Tour

The Cherry Sisters

"The Cherry Sisters" in *Songs in the Key of Z* by Irwin Chusid (Chicago: A Cappella Books, 2000)

Bonnie and Clyde

The Barrow Gang's Visit to Dexter by Debra Sanborn (Dexter, IA: Self-published, 1976)

The Strange History of Bonnie and Clyde by John Treherne (New York: Cooper Square Press, 1984)

The Family Story of Bonnie and Clyde by Phillip W. Steele and Marie Barrow Scoma (Gretna, LA: Pelican Publishing Company, 2000)

Buddy Holly

Buddy Holly: A Biography by Ellis Amburn (New York: St. Martin's Griffin, 1995)

Anita Bryant

A New Day by Anita Bryant (Pigeon Forge, TN: Anita Bryant Publishing, 1996)

Pie Any Means Necessary by the Biotic Baking Brigade (London: AK Press, 2004)

Tom Arnold

How I Lost 5 Pounds in 6 Years by Tom Arnold (New York: St. Martin's Press, 2002)

INDEX BY CITY NAME

Adair

World's First Moving Train Robbery, 2

Algona

The Nazis and Baby Jesus (The Algona Nativity), 4

World's Largest Cheeto, 5

Ames

Insect Zoo, 7

World's First Digital Electronic Computer, 8

World's Largest Rice Krispie Treat, 6

Anamosa

Anamosa State Penitentiary Museum, 64

Captain America's Deathbike (National Motorcycle Museum & Hall of Fame), 65

Arnolds Park

Arnolds Park, 9

Iowa Great Lakes Maritime Museum, 9

The Spirit Lake Massacre, 10

Atlantic

Tractor Day, 83

Audubon

Albert, the World's Largest Bull, 11

Battle Creek

Battle Hill Museum of Natural History, 12

Belle Plaine

George's Filling Station, 67

Boone

Boone & Scenic Valley Railroad, 43

Mamie Doud Eisenhower Birthplace, 13

Brayton

Landmark Tree, 14

Britt

The Hobo Convention and Museum, 15

Brooklyn

The Community of Flags, 68

Burlington

Snake Alley, 146

Burr Oak

The Little Hotel in the Village (Laura Ingalls Wilder Park and Museum), 68

Carlisle

The McCaughey Septuplets, 148

Cedar Falls

Ice Is Nice! (Ice House Museum), 69

Cedar Rapids

Baby Jessica (Court-Sanctioned Kidnapping), 183

The Birth of Bad (The Cherry Sisters), 188

Our Lady of Sorrows Grotto, 71

Tahitian Room and Grizzly Bar (Brucemore), 72

Charles City

Floyd County Historical Society Museum, 83

Clarinda

Birthplace of 4-H (Goldenrod School), 112

Birthplace of Glenn Miller, 112

Clear Lake

The Day the Music Died (Buddy Holly at the Surf Ballroom), 191

Colfax

Trainland U.S.A., 149

Columbus Junction

Lovers Leap Bridge, 151

Coon Rapids

Nikita Khrushchev and the Spinning Ear of Corn (Garst Farm Resorts), 17

Corning

Birthplace of Johnny Carson, 113

Correctionville

The Driftwood Street Jog, 18

Corydon

Jesse James Bank Robbery Site, 3

Council Bluffs

The Angel of Death and Bloomers (Fairview Cemetery), 114

The Big Lake Incident (Big Lake Park), 116

Black Squirrel Town (Bayliss Park), 120

God's Wrath (Broadway United Methodist Church), 116

The Golden Spike, 118

Squirrel Cage Jail (Pottawattamie County Jail), 119

Teeny Tiny House, 121

World's Oldest Dairy Queen, 122

Crescent

Archer Engines of Yesteryear, 123

Creston

Frank Phillips Tourism Information Center, 123

Crystal Lake

World's Largest Bullhead, 19

Davenport

The Brady Street Banshee, 152

Cary Grant's Death Site, 198

The Davenport Stone (Putnam Museum of History and Natural Science), 153

Mother Goose in a Zoo (Fejervary Park Children's Zoo), 155

Palmer College, 156

Decorah

Rocks and Bugs (Porter House Museum), 73

Denison

Donna Reed's Hometown, 20

Earl Marshall, a Lot of Bull, 21

Des Moines

"At least it wasn't fruitcake" (Anita Bryant Pie-in-Face Site), 194

Birthplace of the Roto-Rooter, 96

The Butter Cow Lady (Iowa State Fair), 157

Ozzy Osbourne Bat Biting Site (Veterans Memorial Auditorium), 197

Dexter

Bonnie and Clyde—Ambushed!, 190

Dubuque

    The Fenelon Place Elevator, 74

    Grotto at the Mt. St. Francis Convent, 59

    Mathias Ham House, 76

    World's Largest Ice Cream Sandwich, 6

Dyersville

    Field of Dreams, Fields of Nightmares, 76

    National Farm Toy Museum, 78

Earling

    The Earling Exorcism, 23

East Peru

    Birthplace of the Delicious Apple, 125

Eddyville

    A Headless Treasure, 158

Eldon

    American Gothic House, 160

    Roseanne and Tom's Big Food Diner, 196

Eldora

    Twister House, 79

Elk Horn

    Danish Immigrant Muscum, 24

    Danish Windmill Museum and Welcome Center, 24

Elma

    Viking Throne Chairs, 80

Emmetsburg

    Blarney Stone, 25

Estherville

    The Estherville Meteorite, 26

Exira

    Plow-in-Oak Park, 27

Festina

    World's Smallest Church (St. Anthony of Padua Chapel), 81

Forest City

    Winnebago Birthing Center, 28

Fort Dodge

    A Fake Fake (The Cardiff Giant at the Fort Museum and Frontier Village), 29

Froelich

Birthplace of the Tractor, 82

Fruitland

World's Largest Watermelon Slice, 162

Gladbrook

Matchstick Marvels, 84

Guttenberg

Gutenberg Bible, 84

Hanlontown

Sunset on the Railroad Tracks (Sundown Day), 31

Humboldt

Memorial Fountain at John Brown Park, 59

Ida Grove

Castles and HMS *Bounty*, 32

Indianola

National Balloon Museum, 163

Iowa City

Death to Non-Virgins! (Oakland Cemetery), 164

Jefferson

Ding Dong! (Mahanay Bell Tower), 33

Ring Ring! (Jefferson Telephone Company Museum), 34

Kimballton

The Little Mermaid, 34

Knierim

Bonnie and Clyde Bank Robbery, 191

Knoxville

National Sprint Car Hall of Fame and Museum, 165

Laurens

Fore! (Laurens Golf and Country Club), 35

The Straight Story, 35

Le Mars

Ice Cream Capital of the World, 37

Lockridge

Johnny Clock Museum, 166

Logan

Museum of Religious Arts, 39

Macksburg

National Skillet Throw, 126

Mallard

Big Mallard, 40

Marquette

Pinky the Elephant (Isle of Capri Casino and Hotel), 86

Marshalltown

Big Treehouse, 87

Mason City

Buddy Holly Crash Site, 192

The Day the Music Died (Buddy Holly at the Mason City Airport), 192

"The Lonely Goatherd" Marionettes (Charles H. MacNider Museum), 88

The Music Man (Meredith Willson Boyhood Home and Music Man Square), 89

McGregor

Spook Cave, 92

Missouri Valley

The Sunken *Bertrand*, 127

Mitchell

World's Largest Steam-Powered Tractor (Cedar Valley Memories Museum), 83

Moingona

Kate Shelley Park and Railroad Museum, 42

Kate Shelley, Train Saver (Kate Shelley High Bridge), 41

Montpelier

Varner's Caboose, 167

Mount Ayr

Corny Mural (Mount Ayr Post Office), 128

Muscatine

Pearl Button Museum, 168

Phantasuite Hotel (Econolodge Muscatine Canterbury Hotel), 168

Red Men Speak with Forked Tongue, 170

Nemaha

The Farmall Tractor Promenade, 83

New Hampton

Martha Timm Memorial Rock Garden, 93

Newton

The Day the Boxer Died (Rocky Marciano Crash Site), 193

International Wrestling Institute and Museum, 94

Maytag Historical Center (Jasper County Historical Museum), 95

Onawa

Birthplace of the Eskimo Pie (Monona County Historical Museum), 44

Oskaloosa

Mule Cemetery (Nelson Homestead Pioneer Farm and Craft Museum), 171

Ottumwa

Tom Arnold Escapes, 195

Palo

The Thirteen Steps, 97

Pella

Calvary Wayside Chapel, 172

The Klokkenspel, 173

Pocahontas

World's Largest Pocahontas, 45

Riverside

Future Birthplace of Captain James T. Kirk, 175

Rock Rapids

Bridge to Nowhere (Melan Bridge), 46

Rolfe (Old)

World War II War Memorial, 59

Sac County

World's Largest Popcorn Ball, 6

St. Ansgar

Albino Deer, 98

Shenandoah

Iowa Walk of Fame, 129

Sidney

Worldly Dirt (Fremont County Historical Museum Complex), 130

Sigourney

Open Your Own Museum (Dumont Museum), 177

Sioux City

The Crash of United Flight 232, 47

Eppie and Popo, 48

Lewis & Clark Interpretive Center, 51

Sioux City, continued

Sergeant Floyd River Museum & Welcome Center, 50

Trinity Heights, 49

Unlucky Sergeant Floyd, 50

Witch Hunt, 51

Spillville

The Bily Clocks, 99

Antonín Dvořák Slept Here, 100

Stanhope

Teeny-Weeny Town (Country Relics Village), 53

Stanton

World's Largest Coffee Pot and Coffee Cup Water Towers, 131

Storm Lake

Living Heritage Tree Museum, 55

Strawberry Point

World's Largest Strawberry, 101

Stuart

Bonnie and Clyde Bank Robbery, 191

Tama

Lincoln Highway Bridge, 103

Traer

The Winding Stairs, 104

Vedic City

Maharishi University of Management, 179

Villisca

The Ax Murder House, 133

Walcott

World's Largest Truck Stop, 181

Washta

The Schmidt Tombstones, 56

Waterloo

Sullivan Memorial Park, 104

Waukon

Cowboy and Steer (Village Farm & Home), 106

West Bend

Grotto of the Redemption, 57

West Branch

Herbert Hoover Presidential Library, 106

West Des Moines

First Kid on a Milk Carton, 181

Howard Dean: I Have a Scream (Val Air Ballroom), 199

Weston

Jesse James's Buried Treasure, 3

Winterset

Birthplace of John Wayne, 135

The Bridges of Madison County, 137

Historic Crapper (Madison County Historical Complex), 139

Iowa's Only Tunnel (Pammel State Park), 140

INDEX BY SITE NAME

Albert, the World's Largest Bull, 11

Albino Deer, 98

American Gothic House, 160

Anamosa State Penitentiary Museum, 64

The Angel of Death and Bloomers (Fairview Cemetery), 114

Antonín Dvořák Slept Here, 100

Archer Engines of Yesteryear, 123

Arnolds Park, 9

"At least it wasn't fruitcake" (Anita Bryant Pie-in-Face Site), 194

The Ax Murder House, 133

Baby Jessica (Court-Sanctioned Kidnapping), 183

Battle Hill Museum of Natural History, 12

The Big Lake Incident (Big Lake Park), 116

Big Mallard, 40

Big Treehouse, 87

The Bily Clocks, 99

The Birth of Bad (The Cherry Sisters), 188

Birthplace of 4-H (Goldenrod School), 112

Birthplace of Glenn Miller, 112

Birthplace of John Wayne, 135

Birthplace of Johnny Carson, 113

Birthplace of the Delicious Apple, 125

Birthplace of the Eskimo Pie (Monona County Historical Museum), 44

Birthplace of the Microwave Oven, 96

Birthplace of the Roto-Rooter, 96

Birthplace of the Tractor, 82

Black Squirrel Town (Bayliss Park), 120

Blarney Stone, 25

Bonnie and Clyde—Ambushed!, 190

Bonnie and Clyde Bank Robbery, 191

Boone & Scenic Valley Railroad, 43

The Brady Street Banshee, 152

Bridge to Nowhere (Melan Bridge), 46

The Bridges of Madison County, 137

Buddy Holly Crash Site, 192

The Butter Cow Lady (Iowa State Fair), 157

Calvary Wayside Chapel, 172

Captain America's Deathbike (National Motorcycle Museum & Hall of Fame), 65

Cary Grant's Death Site, 198

Castles and HMS *Bounty*, 32

The Community of Flags, 68

Corny Mural (Mount Ayr Post Office), 128

Cowboy and Steer (Village Farm & Home), 106

The Crash of United Flight 232, 47

Danish Immigrant Museum, 24

Danish Windmill Museum and Welcome Center, 24

The Davenport Stone (Putnam Museum of History and Natural Science), 153

The Day the Boxer Died (Rocky Marciano Crash Site), 193

The Day the Music Died (Buddy Holly at the Mason City Airport), 192

The Day the Music Died (Buddy Holly at the Surf Ballroom), 191

Death to Non-Virgins (Oakland Cemetery), 164

Ding Dong! (Mahanay Bell Tower), 33

Donna Reed's Hometown, 20

The Driftwood Street Jog, 18

Earl Marshall, a Lot of Bull, 21

The Earling Exorcism, 23

Eppie and Popo, 48

The Estherville Meteorite, 26

A Fake Fake (The Cardiff Giant at the Fort Museum and Frontier Village), 29

The Farmall Tractor Promenade, 83

The Fenelon Place Elevator, 74

Field of Dreams, Fields of Nightmares, 76

First Kid on a Milk Carton, 181

Floyd County Historical Society Museum, 83

Fore! (Laurens Golf and Country Club), 35

Frank Phillips Tourism Information Center, 123

Future Birthplace of Captain James T. Kirk, 175

George's Filling Station, 67

God's Wrath (Broadway United Methodist Church), 116

The Golden Spike, 118

Grotto at the Mt. St. Francis Convent, 59

Grotto of the Redemption, 57

Gutenberg Bible, 84

A Headless Treasure, 158

Herbert Hoover Presidential Library, 106

Historic Crapper (Madison County Historical Complex), 139

The Hobo Convention and Museum, 15

Howard Dean: I Have a Scream (Val Air Ballroom), 199

Ice Cream Capital of the World, 37

Ice Is Nice! (Ice House Museum), 69

Insect Zoo, 7

International Wrestling Institute and Museum, 94

Iowa Great Lakes Maritime Museum, 9

Iowa Walk of Fame, 129

Iowa's Only Tunnel (Pammel State Park), 140

Jesse James Bank Robbery Site, 3

Jesse James's Buried Treasure, 3

Johnny Clock Museum, 166

Kate Shelley Park and Railroad Museum, 42

Kate Shelley, Train Saver (Kate Shelley High Bridge), 41

The Klokkenspel, 173

Landmark Tree, 14

Lewis & Clark Interpretive Center, 51

Lincoln Highway Bridge, 103

The Little Mermaid, 34

The Little Hotel in the Village (Laura Ingalls Wilder Park and Museum), 68

Living Heritage Tree Museum, 55

"The Lonely Goatherd" Marionettes (Charles H. MacNider Museum), 88

Lovers Leap Bridge, 151

Maharishi University of Management, 179

Mamie Doud Eisenhower Birthplace, 13

Martha Timm Memorial Rock Garden, 93

Matchstick Marvels, 84

Mathias Ham House, 76

Maytag Historical Center (Jasper County Historical Museum), 95

The McCaughey Septuplets, 148

Memorial Fountain at John Brown Park, 59

Mother Goose in a Zoo (Fejervary Park Children's Zoo), 155

Mule Cemetery (Nelson Homestead Pioneer Farm and Craft Museum), 171

Museum of Religious Arts, 39

The Music Man (Meredith Willson Boyhood Home and Music Man Square), 89

National Balloon Museum, 163

National Farm Toy Museum, 78

National Skillet Throw, 126

National Sprint Car Hall of Fame and Museum, 165

The Nazis and Baby Jesus (The Algona Nativity), 4

Nikita Khrushchev and the Spinning Ear of Corn (Garst Farm Resorts), 17

Open Your Own Museum (Dumont Museum), 177

Our Lady of Sorrows Grotto, 71

Ozzy Osbourne Bat Biting Site (Veterans Memorial Auditorium), 197

Palmer College, 156

Pearl Button Museum, 168

Phantasuite Hotel (Econolodge Muscatine Canterbury Hotel), 168

Pinky the Elephant (Isle of Capri Casino and Hotel), 86

Plow-in-Oak Park, 27

Red Men Speak with Forked Tongue, 170

Ring Ring! (Jefferson Telephone Company Museum), 34

Rocks and Bugs (Porter House Museum), 73

Roseanne and Tom's Big Food Diner, 196

The Schmidt Tombstones, 56

Sergeant Floyd River Museum & Welcome Center, 50

Snake Alley, 146

The Spirit Lake Massacre, 10

Spook Cave, 92

Squirrel Cage Jail (Pottawattamie County Jail), 119

The Straight Story, 35

Sullivan Memorial Park, 104

The Sunken Bertrand, 127

Sunset on the Railroad Tracks (Sundown Day), 31